CREED OR CHAOS?

BOOKS BY DOROTHY L. SAYERS

Detective Stories

IN THE TEETH OF THE EVIDENCE
BUSMAN'S HONEYMOON
GAUDY NIGHT
THE NINE TAILORS

Combined Volumes

MURDER MUST ADVERTISE *and* HANGMAN'S HOLIDAY
STRONG POISON *and* HAVE HIS CARCASE
CLOUDS OF WITNESSES *and* THE DOCUMENTS IN THE CASE
(in collaboration with Robert Eustace)
THE DAWSON PEDIGREE *and* LORD PETER VIEWS THE BODY
WHOSE BODY? THE UNPLEASANTNESS AT THE BELLONA CLUB
and SUSPICIOUS CHARACTERS

Drama

THE ZEAL OF THY HOUSE
THE DEVIL TO PAY

Essays

BEGIN HERE
THE MIND OF THE MAKER
UNPOPULAR OPINIONS
CREED OR CHAOS?

DOROTHY L. SAYERS

Creed or Chaos?

HARCOURT, BRACE AND COMPANY
NEW YORK

Author's Note

THE various articles and speeches included in this volume have all appeared before in pamphlet form, but a number of them have been out of print for a considerable period. Since inquiries are from time to time made for one or other of them, it seemed that it might be a good idea to re-issue them handily under one cover. I have not attempted to remove from them the traces of their occasional origin, such as topical references or the rhythm of the spoken word, but have left them (to use the bookseller's phrase) "with all faults," as originally written or delivered.

D. L. S.

Contents

CREED OR CHAOS?

I. The Greatest Drama Ever Staged

IS THE OFFICIAL CREED OF CHRISTENDOM

OFFICIAL Christianity, of late years, has been having what is known as "a bad press." We are constantly assured that the churches are empty because preachers insist too much upon doctrine—"dull dogma," as people call it. The fact is the precise opposite. It is the neglect of dogma that makes for dullness. The Christian faith is the most exciting drama that ever staggered the imagination of man—and the dogma *is* the drama.

That drama is summarized quite clearly in the creeds of the Church, and if we think it dull it is because we either have never really read those amazing documents, or have recited them so often and so mechanically as to have lost all sense of their meaning. The plot pivots upon a single character, and the whole action is the answer to a single central problem: *What think ye of Christ?* Before we adopt any of the unofficial solutions (some of which are indeed excessively dull)—before we dismiss Christ as a myth, an idealist, a demagogue, a liar, or a lunatic—it will do no harm to find out what the creeds really say about Him. What does the Church think of Christ?

The Church's answer is categorical and uncompromising, and it is this: That Jesus Bar-Joseph, the carpenter of Nazareth, was in fact and in truth, and in the most exact and literal sense of the words, the God "by whom all things were made." His body and brain were those of a common man; His personality was the personality of God, so far as that personality could be expressed in human terms. He was not a kind of demon or fairy pretending to be human;

He was in every respect a genuine living man. He was not merely a man so good as to be "like God"—He *was* God.

Now, this is not just a pious commonplace; it is not commonplace at all. For what it means is this, among other things: that for whatever reason God chose to make man as he is—limited and suffering and subject to sorrows and death—He had the honesty and the courage to take His own medicine. Whatever game He is playing with His creation, He has kept His own rules and played fair. He can exact nothing from man that He has not exacted from Himself. He has Himself gone through the whole of human experience, from the trivial irritations of family life and the cramping restrictions of hard work and lack of money to the worst horrors of pain and humiliation, defeat, despair, and death. When He was a man, He played the man. He was born in poverty and died in disgrace and thought it well worth while.

Christianity is, of course, not the only religion that has found the best explanation of human life in the idea of an incarnate and suffering god. The Egyptian Osiris died and rose again; Aeschylus in his play, *The Eumenides,* reconciled man to God by the theory of a suffering Zeus. But in most theologies, the god is supposed to have suffered and died in some remote and mythical period of pre-history. The Christian story, on the other hand, starts off briskly in St. Matthew's account with a place and a date: "When Jesus was born in Bethlehem of Judea in the days of Herod the King." St. Luke, still more practically and prosaically, pins the thing down by a reference to a piece of government finance. God, he says, was made man in the year when Caesar Augustus was taking a census in connexion with a scheme of taxation. Similarly, we might date an event by saying that it took place in the year that Great Britain went off the gold standard. About thirty-three years later (we are informed) God was executed, for being a political nuisance, "under Pontius Pilate"—much as we might say, "when Mr. Joynson-Hicks was Home Secretary." It is as definite and concrete as all that.

Possibly we might prefer not to take this tale too seriously —there are disquieting points about it. Here we had a man of Divine character walking and talking among us—and what did we find to do with Him? The common people, indeed, "heard Him gladly"; but our leading authorities in Church and State considered that He talked too much and uttered too many disconcerting truths. So we bribed one of His friends to hand Him over quietly to the police, and we tried Him on a rather vague charge of creating a disturbance, and had Him publicly flogged and hanged on the common gallows, "thanking God we were rid of a knave." All this was not very creditable to us, even if He was (as many people thought and think) only a harmless crazy preacher. But if the Church is right about Him, it was more discreditable still; for the man we hanged was God Almighty.

So that is the outline of the official story—the tale of the time when God was the under-dog and got beaten, when He submitted to the conditions He had laid down and became a man like the men He had made, and the men He had made broke Him and killed Him. This is the dogma we find so dull—this terrifying drama of which God is the victim and hero.

If this is dull, then what, in Heaven's name, is worthy to be called exciting? The people who hanged Christ never, to do them justice, accused Him of being a bore—on the contrary; they thought Him too dynamic to be safe. It has been left for later generations to muffle up that shattering personality and surround Him with an atmosphere of tedium. We have very efficiently pared the claws of the Lion of Judah, certified Him "meek and mild," and recommended Him as a fitting household pet for pale curates and pious old ladies. To those who knew Him, however, He in no way suggested a milk-and-water person; *they* objected to Him as a dangerous firebrand. True, He was tender to the unfortunate, patient with honest inquirers, and humble before Heaven; but He insulted respectable clergymen by calling them hypocrites; He referred to King Herod as "that fox"; He went to parties in disreputable company and was looked upon as a "gluttonous man and a wine-bibber, a friend of publicans and sinners"; He assaulted indignant tradesmen and threw them and their belongings out of the Temple; He drove a coach-and-horses through a number of sacrosanct and hoary regulations; He cured diseases by any means that came handy, with a shocking casualness in the matter of other people's pigs and property; He showed no proper deference for wealth or social position; when confronted with neat dialectical traps, He displayed a paradoxical humour that affronted serious-minded people, and He retorted by asking disagreeably searching questions that could not be answered by rule of thumb. He was emphatically not a dull man in His human lifetime, and if He was God, there can be nothing dull about God either. But He had "a daily beauty in His life that made us ugly," and officialdom felt that the established order of things would be more secure without Him. So they did away with God in the name of peace and quietness.

"And the third day He rose again"; what are we to make of that? One thing is certain: if He was God and nothing else, His immortality means nothing to us; if He was man and no more, His death is no more important than yours or mine. But if He really was both God and man, then when the man Jesus died, God died too, and when the God Jesus rose from the dead, man rose too, because they were one and the same person. The Church binds us to no theory about the exact composition of Christ's Resurrection Body. A body of some kind there had to be, since man cannot perceive the Infinite otherwise than in terms of space and time. It may have been made from the same elements as the body that disappeared so strangely from the guarded tomb, but it was not that old, limited, mortal body, though it was recognizably like it. In any case, those who saw the risen Christ remained persuaded that life was worth living and death a triviality—an attitude curiously unlike that of the modern defeatist, who is firmly persuaded that life is a

disaster and death (rather inconsistently) a major catastrophe.

Now, nobody is compelled to believe a single word of this
remarkable story. God (says the Church) has created us
perfectly free to disbelieve in Him as much as we choose.
If we do disbelieve, then He and we must take the consequences in a world ruled by cause and effect. The Church
says further, that man did, in fact, disbelieve, and that God
did, in fact, take the consequences. All the same, if we are
going to disbelieve a thing, it seems on the whole to be
desirable that we should first find out what, exactly, we are
disbelieving. Very well, then: "The right Faith is, that we
believe that Jesus Christ is God *and* Man. Perfect God and
perfect Man, of a reasonable soul and human flesh subsist-
ing. Who although He be God and Man, yet is He not two,
but one Christ." There is the essential doctrine, of which
the whole elaborate structure of Christian faith and morals
is only the logical consequence.

Now, we may call that doctrine exhilarating or we may
call it devastating; we may call it revelation or we may call
it rubbish; but if we call it dull, then words have no meaning at all. That God should play the tyrant over man is a
dismal story of unrelieved oppression; that man should play
the tyrant over man is the usual dreary record of human
futility; but that man should play the tyrant over God and
find Him a better man than himself is an astonishing drama
indeed. Any journalist, hearing of it for the first time,
would recognize it as News; those who did hear it for the
first time actually called it News, and good news at that;
though we are apt to forget that the word Gospel ever
meant anything so sensational.

Perhaps the drama is played out now, and Jesus is safely
dead and buried. Perhaps. It is ironical and entertaining
to consider that once at least in the world's history those
words might have been spoken with complete conviction,
and that was upon the eve of the Resurrection.

II. The Triumph of Easter

"O felix culpa!" said Augustine of Hippo, rather danger-ously, with reference to the sin of Adam. "O happy guilt, that did deserve such and so great a Redeemer!"

It is difficult, perhaps, to imagine a pronouncement that lays itself more open to misunderstanding. It is the kind of paradox that bishops and clergy are warned to beware of uttering from the pulpit. But, then, the Bishop of Hippo was a very remarkable bishop indeed, with a courage of his convictions rare in highly placed ecclesiastical persons.

If spiritual pastors are to refrain from saying anything that might ever, by any possibility, be misunderstood by anybody, they will end—as in fact many of them do—by never saying anything worth hearing. Incidentally, this particular brand of timidity is the besetting sin of the good churchman. Not that the Church approves it. She knows it of old for a part of the great, sprawling, drowsy, deadly Sin of Sloth—a sin from which the preachers of fads, schisms, heresies, and anti-Christ are most laudably free.

The children of this world are not only (as Christ so caustically observed) wiser in their generation than the children of light; they are also more energetic, more stimu-lating and bolder. It is always, of course, more amusing to attack than to defend; but good Christian people should have learnt by now that it is best to defend by attacking, seeing that the Kingdom of Heaven suffereth violence, and the violent take it by force. St. Augustine, anyway, seeing the perpetual problem of sin and evil being brought up and planted, like a battery, against the Christian position, sal-lied promptly forth, like the good strategist he was, and spiked its guns with a thanksgiving.

The problem of sin and evil is, as everybody knows, one

8

which all religions have to face, especially those that postulate an all-good and all-powerful God. "If," we say readily, "God is holy and omnipotent, He would interfere and stop all this kind of thing"—meaning by "this kind of thing" wars, persecutions, cruelties, Hitlerism, Bolshevism, or whatever large issue happens to be distressing our minds at the time. But let us be quite sure that we have really considered the problem in all its aspects.

"Why doesn't God smite this dictator dead?" is a question a little remote from us. Why, madam, did He not strike you dumb and imbecile before you uttered that baseless and unkind slander the day before yesterday? Or me, before I behaved with such cruel lack of consideration to that well-meaning friend? And why, sir, did He not cause your hand to rot off at the wrist before you signed your name to that dirty little bit of financial trickery?

You did not quite mean that? But why not? Your misdeeds and mine are none the less repellent because our opportunities for doing damage are less spectacular than those of some other people. Do you suggest that your doings and mine are too trivial for God to bother about? That cuts both ways; for, in that case, it would make precious little difference to His creation if He wiped us both out tomorrow.

Well, perhaps that is not quite what we meant. We meant why did God create His universe on these lines at all? Why did He not make us mere puppets, incapable of executing anything but His own pattern of perfection? Some schools of thought assert that He did, that everything we do (including Jew-baiting in Germany and our own disgusting rudeness to Aunt Eliza) is rigidly determined for us, and that, however much we may dislike the pattern, we can do nothing about it. This is one of those theories that are supposed to free us from the trammels of superstition. It certainly relieves our minds of all responsibility; unfortunately, it imposes a fresh set of trammels of its own. Also, however much we may believe in it, we seem forced to behave as though we did not.

Christians (surprising as it may appear) are not the only people who fail to act up to their creed; for what determinist philosopher, when his breakfast bacon is uneatable, will not blame the free will of the cook, like any Christian? To be sure, the philosopher's protest, like his bacon, is predetermined also; that is the silly part of it. Our minds are the material we have to work upon when constructing philosophies, and it seems but an illogical creed, whose proof depends on our discarding all the available evidence.

The Church, at any rate, says that man's will is free, and that evil is the price we pay for knowledge, particularly the kind of knowledge which we call self-consciousness. It follows that we can, by God's grace, do something about the pattern. Moreover, God Himself, says the Church, is doing something about it—with our co-operation, if we choose, in despite of us if we refuse to co-operate—but always, steadily, working the pattern out.

And here we come up against the ultimate question which no theology, no philosophy, no theory of the universe has ever so much as attempted to answer completely. Why should God, if there is a God, create anything, at any time, of any kind at all? That is a real mystery, and probably the only completely insoluble mystery there is. The one person who might be able to give some sort of guess at the answer is the creative artist, and he, of all people in the world, is the least inclined even to ask the question, being accustomed to take all creative activity as its own sufficient justification.

But we may all, perhaps, allow that it is easier to believe the universe to have come into existence for some reason than for no reason at all. The Church asserts that there is a Mind which made the universe, that He made it because He is the sort of Mind that takes pleasure in creation, and that if we want to know what the Mind of the Creator is, we must look at Christ. In Him, we shall discover a Mind that loved His own creation so completely that He became part of it, suffered with and for it, and made it a sharer in His own glory and a fellow-worker with Himself in the working out of His own design for it.

That is the bold postulate that the Church asks us to accept, adding that, if we do accept it (and every theoretical scheme demands the acceptance of some postulate or other) the answers to all our other problems will be found to make sense.

Accepting the postulate, then, and looking at Christ, what do we find God "doing about" this business of sin and evil? And what is He expecting us to do about it? Here, the Church is clear enough. We find God continually at work turning evil into good. Not, as a rule, by irrelevant miracles and theatrically effective judgments—Christ was seldom very encouraging to those who demanded signs, or lightnings from Heaven, and God is too subtle and too economical a craftsman to make very much use of those methods. But He takes our sins and errors and turns them into victories, as He made the crime of the crucifixion to be the salvation of the world. *"O felix culpa!"* exclaimed St. Augustine, contemplating the accomplished work.

Here is the place where we are exceedingly liable to run into misunderstanding. God does not need our sin, still less does He make us sin, in order to demonstrate His power and glory. His is not the uneasy power that has to reassure itself by demonstrations. Nor is it desirable that we should create evils on purpose for the fun of seeing Him put them right. That is not the idea at all. Nor yet are we to imagine that evil does not matter, since God can make it all right in the long run.

Whatever the Church preaches on this point, it is *not* a facile optimism. And it is *not* the advisability of doing evil that good may come. Over-simplification of this sort is as misleading as too much complication and just as perilously attractive. It is, for instance, startling and illuminating to hear a surgeon say casually, when congratulated upon some miracle of healing, "Of course, we couldn't have done that operation without the experience we gained in the War."

There is a good result of evil; but, even if the number of sufferers healed were to exceed that of all the victims who suffered in the War, does that allay the pangs of the victims or of any one of them, or excuse the guilt that makes war possible? No, says the Church, it does not. If an artist discovers that the experience gained through his worst sins enables him to produce his best work, does that entitle him to live like a beast for the sake of his art? No, says the Church, it does not. We can behave as badly as we like, but we cannot escape the consequences. "Take what you will, said God" (according to the Spanish proverb), "take it and pay for it." Or somebody else may do the paying and pay fully, willingly, and magnificently, but the debt is still ours. "The Son of man goeth as it is written of Him; but woe unto that man by whom the Son of man is betrayed! it had been good for that man if he had not been born."

When Judas sinned, Jesus paid; He brought good out of evil, He led out triumph from the gates of hell and brought all mankind out with Him; but the suffering of Jesus and the sin of Judas remain a reality. God did not abolish the fact of evil: He transformed it. He did not stop the crucifixion: He rose from the dead.

"Then Judas which had betrayed Him, when he saw that He was condemned . . . cast down the pieces of silver in the temple, and departed, and went and hanged himself." And thereby Judas committed the final, the fatal, the most pitiful error of all; for he despaired of God and himself and never waited to see the Resurrection. Had he done so, there would have been an encounter, and an opportunity, to leave invention bankrupt; but unhappily for himself, he did not. In this world, at any rate, he never saw the triumph of Christ fulfilled upon him, and through him, and despite of him. He saw the dreadful payment made, and never knew what victory had been purchased with the price.

All of us, perhaps, are too ready, when our behaviour turns out to have appalling consequences, to rush out and hang ourselves. Sometimes we do worse, and show an inclination to go and hang other people. Judas, at least, seems to have blamed nobody but himself, and St. Peter, who had a minor betrayal of his own to weep for, made his act of contrition and waited to see what came next. What came next for St. Peter and the other disciples was the sudden assurance of what God was, and with it the answer to all the riddles.

If Christ could take evil and suffering and do that sort of thing with them, then of course it was all worth while, and the triumph of Easter linked up with that strange, triumphant prayer in the Upper Room, which the events of Good Friday had seemed to make so puzzling. As for their own parts in the drama, nothing could now alter the fact that they had been stupid, cowardly, faithless, and in many ways singularly unhelpful; but they did not allow any morbid and egotistical remorse to inhibit their joyful activities in the future.

Now, indeed, they could go out and "do something" about the problem of sin and suffering. They had seen the strong hands of God twist the crown of thorns into a crown of glory, and in hands as strong as that they knew themselves safe. They had misunderstood practically everything Christ had ever said to them, but no matter: the thing made sense at last, and the meaning was far beyond anything they had dreamed. They had expected a walk-over, and they beheld a victory; they had expected an earthly Messiah, and they beheld the Soul of Eternity.

It had been said to them of old time, "No man shall look upon My face and live"; but for them a means had been found. They had seen the face of the living God turned upon them; and it was the face of a suffering and rejoicing Man.

III.   Strong Meat

For every one that useth milk is unskilful in the word of righteousness; for he is a babe.

But strong meat belongeth to them that are of full age, even those who by reason of use have their senses exercised to discern both good and evil.—EPISTLE TO THE HEBREWS.

IT is over twenty years since I first read the words, in some forgotten book. I remember neither the name of the author, nor that of the saint from whose meditations he was quoting.* Only the statement itself has survived the accidents of transmission: *"Cibus sum grandium; cresce, et manducabis Me"*—"I am the food of the full-grown; become a man, and thou shalt feed on Me."

Here is a robust assertion of the claim of Christianity to be a religion for adult minds. I am glad to think, *now,* that it impressed me so forcibly *then,* when I was still comparatively young. To protest, when one has left one's youth behind, against the prevalent assumption that there is no salvation for the middle-aged is all very well; but it is apt to provoke a mocking reference to the fox who lost his tail. One is in a stronger position if one can show that one had already registered the protest before circumstances rendered it expedient.

There is a popular school of thought (or, more strictly, of feeling) which violently resents the operation of Time upon the human spirit. It looks upon age as something between a crime and an insult. Its prophets have banished from their savage vocabulary all such words as "adult," "mature," "experienced," "venerable"; they know only snarling and sneering epithets, like "middle-aged," "elderly," "stuffy," "senile," and "decrepit." With these they

* But I would have laid any odds, from the style, that it was Augustine of Hippo; and so, indeed, it proves to be (*Confessions,* vii. 10).

flagellate that which they themselves are, or must shortly become, as though abuse were an incantation to exorcize the inexorable. Theirs is neither the thoughtless courage that "makes mouths at the invisible event," nor the reasoned courage that foresees the event and endures it; still less is it the ecstatic courage that embraces and subdues the event. It is the vicious and desperate fury of a trapped beast; and it is not a pretty sight.

Such men, finding no value for the world as it is, proclaim very loudly their faith in the future, "which is in the hands of the young." With this flattery, they bind their own burden on the shoulders of the next generation. For their own failures, Time alone is to blame—not Sin, which is expiable, but Time, which is irreparable. From the relentless reality of age they seek escape into a fantasy of youth—their own or other people's. First love, boyhood ideals, childish dreams, the song at the mother's breast, the blind security of the womb—from these they construct a monstrous fabric of pretence, to be their hiding-place from the tempest. Their faith is not really in the future, but in the past. Paradoxical as it may seem, to believe in youth is to look backward; to look forward, we must believe in age.

"Except," said Christ, "ye become as little children"—and the words are sometimes quoted to justify the flight into infantilism. Now, children differ in many ways, but they have one thing in common. Peter Pan—if indeed he exists otherwise than in the nostalgic imagination of an adult—is a case for the pathologist. All normal children (however much we discourage them) look forward to growing up. "Except ye become as little children," except you can wake on your fiftieth birthday with the same forward-looking excitement and interest in life that you enjoyed when you were five, "ye cannot see the Kingdom of God." One must not only die daily, but every day one must be born again.

"How can a man be born when he is old?" asked Nicodemus. His question has been ridiculed; but it is very reasonable and even profound. "Can he enter a second time into his mother's womb and be born?" Can he escape from

Time, creep back into the comfortable pre-natal darkness, renounce the values of experience? The answer makes short work of all such fantasies. "That which is born of the flesh is flesh, and that which is born of the Spirit is spirit." The spirit alone is eternal youth; the mind and the body must learn to make terms with Time.

Time is a difficult subject for thought, because in a sense we know too much about it. It is perhaps the only phenomenon of which we have direct apprehension; if all our senses were destroyed, we should still remain aware of duration. Moreover, all conscious thought is a process in time; so that to think consciously about Time is like trying to use a foot-rule to measure its own length. The awareness of timelessness, which some people have, does not belong to the order of conscious thought and cannot be directly expressed in the language of conscious thought, which is temporal. For every conscious human purpose (including thought) we are compelled to reckon (in every sense of the word) with Time.

Now, the Christian Church has always taken a thoroughly realistic view of Time, and has been very particular to distinguish between Time and Eternity. In her view of the matter, Time is not an aspect or a fragment of Eternity, nor is Eternity an endless extension of Time; the two concepts belong to different categories. Both have a divine reality: God is the Ancient of Days and also the I AM: the Everlasting, and also the Eternal Present; the Logos and also the Father; the Creeds, with their usual practicality, issue a sharp warning that we shall get into a nasty mess if we confuse the two or deny the reality of either. Moreover, the mystics—those rare spirits who are simultaneously aware of Time and Eternity—support the doctrine by their knowledge and example. They are never vague, woolly-minded people to whom Time means nothing; on the contrary, they insist more than anybody upon the validity of Time and the actuality of human experience.

The reality of Time is not affected by considering it as a dimension in a space-time continuum or as a solid having dimensions of its own. "There's a great devil in the universe," says Kay in *Time and the Conways,* "and we call it Time. . . . If things were merely mixed—good and bad—that would be all right, but they get worse. . . . Time's beating us." Her brother replies that Time is "only a kind of dream," and that the "happy young Conways of the past" are still real and existing. "We're seeing another bit of the view—a bad bit if you like—but the whole landscape's still there. . . . At this moment, or any moment, we're only a cross-section of our real selves. What we *really* are is the whole stretch of ourselves, all our time, and when we come to the end of this life, all our time will be *us*—the real you, the real me."

Granted all this—that the happy young Conways still co-exist, *now,* with the unhappy, middle-aged Conways; granted also the converse—that the unhappy, middle-aged Conways already co-existed, *then,* with the happy young Conways. What of it? All we have done is to substitute a spatial image for a temporal one. Instead of a *progress* from good to evil we have a *prospect* (or "landscape") of mixed good and evil, which, viewed in its entirety ("when we come to the end of this life") must necessarily contain more evil than good, since things "get worse and worse." Kay may find this "all right"; the fact remains that there is here no conquest over Time, but an unconditional surrender.

That surrender is made in the moment when we assume that Time is evil in itself and brings nothing but deterioration. It is a pity that the Conway family contained no saint, no artist, no one who had achieved any measure of triumphant fulfilment. His opinion would have been of great interest, since he might have spoken with authority of the soul's development in Time, of the vigorous grappling with evil that transforms it into good, of the dark night of the soul that precedes crucifixion and issues in resurrection.

In contending with the problem of evil it is useless to try to escape either *from* the bad past or *into* the good past. The only way to deal with the past is to accept the *whole* past, and by accepting it, to change its meaning. The hero

of T. S. Eliot's *The Family Reunion,* haunted by the guilt
of a hereditary evil, seeks at first "To creep back through
the little door" into the shelter of the unaltered past, and
finds no refuge there from the pursuing hounds of heaven.
"Now I know That the last apparent refuge, the safe shelter, That is where one meets them; that is the way of
spectres. . . ." So long as he flees from Time and Evil he is
thrall to them, not till he welcomes them does he find
strength to transmute them. "And now I know That my
business is not to run away, but to pursue, Not to avoid
being found, but to seek. . . . It is at once the hardest
thing, and the only thing possible. Now they will lead me;
I shall be safe with them. I am not safe there. . . . I must
follow the bright angels." Then, and only then, is he en-
abled to apprehend the good in the evil and to see the ter-
rible hunters of the soul in their true angelic shape. "I feel
quite happy, as if happiness Did not consist in getting what
one wanted, Or in getting rid of what can't be got rid of,
But in a different vision." It is the release, not from, but
into, Reality.

This is the great way of Christian acceptance—a very
different thing from so-called "Christian" resignation,
which merely submits without ecstasy. "Repentance," says
a Christian writer,* "is no more than a passionate intention to know all things after the mode of Heaven, and it is
impossible to know evil as good if you insist on knowing it
as evil." For man's evil knowledge, "there could be but one
perfect remedy—to know the evil of the past itself as good,
and to be free from the necessity of evil in the future—to
find right knowledge and perfect freedom together; to know
all things as occasions of love."

The story of Passion-Tide and Easter is the story of the
winning of that freedom and of that victory over the evils
of Time. The burden of the guilt is accepted ("He was
made Sin"), the last agony of alienation from God is passed
through (*Eloi, lama sabachthani*); the temporal Body is

* Charles Williams: *He Came Down from Heaven.*

broken and remade; and Time and Eternity are reconciled in a Single Person. There is no retreat here to the Paradise of primal ignorance; the new Kingdom of God is built upon the foundations of spiritual experience. Time is not denied; it is fulfilled. "I am the food of the full-grown."

IV. The Dogma Is the Drama

"ANY stigma," said a witty tongue, "will do to beat a dogma"; and the flails of ridicule have been brandished with such energy of late on the threshing-floor of controversy that the true seed of the Word has become well-nigh lost amid the whirling of chaff. Christ, in His Divine innocence, said to the Woman of Samaria, "Ye worship ye know not what"—being apparently under the impression that it might be desirable, on the whole, to know what one was worshipping. He thus showed Himself sadly out of touch with the twentieth-century mind, for the cry today is: "Away with the tedious complexities of dogma—let us have the simple spirit of worship; just worship, no matter of what!" The only drawback to this demand for a generalized and undirected worship is the practical difficulty of arousing any sort of enthusiasm for the worship of nothing in particular.

It would not perhaps be altogether surprising if, in this nominally Christian country, where the Creeds are daily recited, there were a number of people who knew all about Christian doctrine and disliked it. It is more startling to discover how many people there are who heartily dislike and despise Christianity without having the faintest notion what it is. If you tell them, they cannot believe you. I do not mean that they cannot believe the doctrine: that would be understandable enough, since it takes some believing. I mean that they simply cannot believe that anything so interesting, so exciting, and so dramatic can be the orthodox Creed of the Church.

That this is really the case was made plain to me by the questions asked me, mostly by young men, about my Canterbury play, *The Zeal of Thy House*. The action of the play involves a dramatic presentation of a few fundamental

Christian dogmas—in particular, the application to human affairs of the doctrine of the Incarnation. That the Church believed Christ to be in any *real* sense God, or that the Eternal Word was supposed to be associated in any way with the work of Creation; that Christ was held to be at the same time Man in any *real* sense of the word; that the doctrine of the Trinity could be considered to have any relation to fact or any bearing on psychological truth; that the Church considered Pride to be sinful, or indeed took notice of any sin beyond the more disreputable sins of the flesh:—all these things were looked upon as astonishing and revolutionary novelties, imported into the Faith by the feverish imagination of a playwright. I protested in vain against this flattering tribute to my powers of invention, referring my inquirers to the Creeds, to the Gospels, and to the offices of the Church; I insisted that if my play was dramatic it was so, not in spite of the dogma but because of it—that, in short, the dogma *was* the drama. The explanation was, however, not well received; it was felt that if there was anything attractive in Christian philosophy I must have put it there myself.

Judging by what my young friends tell me, and also by what is said on the subject in anti-Christian literature written by people who ought to have taken a little trouble to find out what they are attacking before attacking it, I have come to the conclusion that a short examination paper on the Christian religion might be very generally answered as follows:

Q.: What does the Church think of God the Father?

A.: He is omnipotent and holy. He created the world and imposed on man conditions impossible of fulfilment; He is very angry if these are not carried out. He sometimes interferes by means of arbitrary judgments and miracles, distributed with a good deal of favouritism. He likes to be truckled to and is always ready to pounce on anybody who trips up over a difficulty in the Law, or is having a bit of fun. He is rather like a dictator, only larger and more arbitrary.

Q.: What does the Church think of God the Son?

A.: He is in some way to be identified with Jesus of Nazareth. It was not His fault that the world was made like this, and, unlike God the Father, He is friendly to man and did His best to reconcile man to God (see *Atonement*). He has a good deal of influence with God, and if you want anything done, it is best to apply to Him.

Q.: What does the Church think of God the Holy Ghost?

A.: I don't know exactly. He was never seen or heard of till Whit-Sunday. There is a sin against Him which damns you for ever, but nobody knows what it is.

Q.: What is the doctrine of the Trinity?

A.: "The Father incomprehensible, the Son incomprehensible, and the whole thing incomprehensible." Something put in by theologians to make it more difficult—nothing to do with daily life or ethics.

Q.: What was Jesus Christ like in real life?

A.: He was a good man—so good as to be called the Son of God. He is to be identified in some way with God the Son (q.v.). He was meek and mild and preached a simple religion of love and pacifism. He had no sense of humour. Anything in the Bible that suggests another side to His character must be an interpolation, or a paradox invented by G. K. Chesterton. If we try to live like Him, God the Father will let us off being damned hereafter and only have us tortured in this life instead.

Q.: What is meant by the Atonement?

A.: God wanted to damn everybody, but His vindictive sadism was sated by the crucifixion of His own Son, who was quite innocent, and, therefore, a particularly attractive victim. He now only damns people who don't follow Christ or who never heard of Him.

Q.: What does the Church think of sex?

A.: God made it necessary to the machinery of the world, and tolerates it, provided the parties (*a*) are married, and (*b*) get no pleasure out of it.

Q.: What does the Church call Sin?

A.: Sex (otherwise than as excepted above); getting

drunk; saying "damn"; murder, and cruelty to dumb ani-
mals; not going to church; most kinds of amusement. "Original sin" means that anything we enjoy doing is wrong.

Q.: What is faith?

A.: Resolutely shutting your eyes to scientific fact.

Q.: What is the human intellect?

A.: A barrier to faith.

Q.: What are the seven Christian virtues?

A.: Respectability; childishness; mental timidity; dullness; sentimentality; censoriousness; and depression of
spirits.

Q.: Wilt thou be baptized in this faith?

A.: No fear!

I cannot help feeling that as a statement of Christian
orthodoxy, these replies are inadequate, if not misleading.
But I also cannot help feeling that they do fairly accurately
represent what many people take Christian orthodoxy to be,
and for this state of affairs I am inclined to blame the
orthodox. Whenever an average Christian is represented in
a novel or a play, he is pretty sure to be shown practising
one or all of the Seven Deadly Virtues enumerated above,
and I am afraid that this is the impression made by the
average Christian upon the world at large.

Perhaps we are not following Christ all the way or in
quite the right spirit. We are apt, for example, to be a little
sparing of the palms and the hosannas. We are chary of
wielding the scourge of small cords, lest we should offend
somebody or interfere with trade. We do not furbish up
our wits to disentangle knotty questions about Sunday ob-
servance and tribute-money, nor hasten to sit at the feet
of the doctors, both hearing them and asking them questions. We pass hastily over disquieting jests about making
friends the mammon of unrighteousness and alarming observations about bringing not peace but a sword; nor
do we distinguish ourselves by the graciousness with which
we sit at meat with publicans and sinners. Somehow or
other, and with the best intentions, we have shown the
world the typical Christian in the likeness of a crashing and

rather ill-natured bore—and this in the Name of One who assuredly never bored a soul in those thirty-three years during which He passed through the world like a flame.

Let us, in Heaven's name, drag out the Divine Drama from under the dreadful accumulation of slipshod thinking and trashy sentiment heaped upon it, and set it on an open stage to startle the world into some sort of vigorous reaction. If the pious are the first to be shocked, so much the worse for the pious—others will pass into the Kingdom of Heaven before them. If all men are offended because of Christ, let them be offended; but where is the sense of their being offended at something that is not Christ and is nothing like Him? We do Him singularly little honour by watering down His personality till it could not offend a fly. Surely it is not the business of the Church to adapt Christ to men, but to adapt men to Christ.

It is the dogma that is the drama—not beautiful phrases, nor comforting sentiments, nor vague aspirations to loving-kindness and uplift, nor the promise of something nice after death—but the terrifying assertion that the same God who made the world lived in the world and passed through the grave and gate of death. Show that to the heathen, and they may not believe it; but at least they may realize that here is something that a man might be glad to believe.

V. Creed or Chaos? *

And when he is come, he will convict the world of sin, and of righteousness, and of judgment: of sin, because they believe not on me; of righteousness, because I go to the Father, and ye see me no more; of judgment, because the prince of this world is judged.—ST. JOHN xvi. 8-11.

SOMETHING is happening to us today which has not happened for a very long time. We are waging a war of religion. Not a civil war between adherents of the same religion, but a life-and-death struggle between Christian and pagan. The Christians are, it must be confessed, not very good Christians, and the pagans do not officially proclaim themselves worshippers of Mahound or even of Odin, but the stark fact remains that Christendom and heathendom now stand face to face as they have not done in Europe since the days of Charlemagne. In spite of the various vague references in sermons and public speeches to the War as a "crusade," I think we have scarcely begun to realize the full implications of this. It is a phenomenon of quite extraordinary importance. The people who say that this is a war of economics or of power-politics, are only dabbling about on the surface of things. Even those who say it is a war to preserve freedom and justice and faith have gone only halfway to the truth. The real question is what economics and politics are to be used for; whether freedom and justice and faith have any right to be considered at all; at bottom it is a violent and irreconcilable quarrel about the nature of God and the nature of man and the ultimate nature of the universe; it is a war of dogma.

The word dogma is unpopular, and that is why I have used it. It is our own distrust of dogma that is handicap-

* An address delivered at Derby, England, May 4, 1940.

ping us in the struggle. The immense spiritual strength of our opponents lies precisely in the fact that they have fervently embraced, and hold with fanatical fervour, a dogma which is none the less a dogma for being called an "ideology." We on our side have been trying for several centuries to uphold a particular standard of ethical values which derives from Christian dogma, while gradually dispensing with the very dogma which is the sole rational foundation for those values. The rulers of Germany have seen quite clearly that dogma and ethics are inextricably bound together. Having renounced the dogma, they have renounced the ethics as well—and from their point of view they are perfectly right. They have adopted an entirely different dogma, whose ethical scheme has no value for peace or truth, mercy or justice, faith or freedom; and they see no reason why they should practise a set of virtues incompatible with their dogma.

We have been very slow to understand this. We persist in thinking that Germany "really" believes those things to be right that we believe to be right, and is only very naughty in her behaviour. That is a thing we find quite familiar. We often do wrong things, knowing them to be wrong. For a long time we kept on imagining that if we granted certain German demands which seemed fairly reasonable, she would stop being naughty and behave according to our ideas of what was right and proper. We still go on scolding Germany for disregarding the standard of European ethics, as though that standard was something which she still acknowledged. It is only with great difficulty that we can bring ourselves to grasp the fact that there is no failure in Germany to live up to her own standards of right conduct. It is something much more terrifying and tremendous: it is that what we believe to be evil, Germany believes to be good. It is a direct repudiation of the basic Christian dogma on which our Mediterranean civilization, such as it is, is grounded.

I do not want now to discuss the ideology of Germany, nor yet that of Russia which, in rather a different way, is also a repudiation of Christendom. Nor do I want to talk about our own war-aims and peace-aims, and how far we are single-minded about them. All I want to say on this point is that, however deeply we have sinned—and God knows we have done plenty of evil in our time—we have not gone so far as to have altogether lost all claim to stand for Christendom. There is a great difference between believing a thing to be right and not doing it, on the one hand, and, on the other, energetically practising evil in the firm conviction that it is good. In theological language, the one is mortal sin, which is bad enough; the other is the sin against the Holy Ghost, which is without forgiveness simply and solely because the sinner has not the remotest idea that he is sinning at all. So long as we are aware that we are wicked, we are not corrupt beyond all hope. Our present dissatisfaction with ourselves is a good sign. We have only to be careful that we do not get too disheartened and abashed to do anything about it all.

The only reason why I have mentioned Germany is this: that in the present conflict we have before us, in a visible and physical form which we cannot possibly overlook, the final consequences of a quarrel about dogma. A quarrel of that kind can go on for a very long time beneath the surface, and we can ignore it so long as disagreement about dogma is not translated into physical terms. While there is a superficial consensus of opinion about the ethics of behaviour, we can easily persuade ourselves that the underlying dogma is immaterial. We can, as we cheerfully say, "agree to differ." "Never mind about theology," we observe in kindly tones, "if we just go on being brotherly to one another it doesn't matter what we believe about God." We are so accustomed to this idea that we are not perturbed by the man who demands: "If I do not believe in the fatherhood of God, why should I believe in the brotherhood of man?" That, we think, is an interesting point of view, but it is only talk—a subject for quiet after-dinner discussion. But if the man goes on to translate his point of view into action, then, to our horror and surprise, the foundations of society are violently shaken, the crust of morality that looked so solid splits apart, and we see that it was only a thin bridge over an abyss in which two dogmas, incompatible as fire and water, are seething explosively together.

Now in this assembly I may take it for granted that we are generally agreed as to what is good and what is evil. However little we may have lived up to our beliefs, I take it that we are ready, if challenged, to cry, like the paladins in the *Song of Roland:*

Paiens unt tort e Chrestiens unt dreit

(Pagans are wrong, Christians are in the right.)

The thing I am here to say to you is this: that it is worse than useless for Christians to talk about the importance of Christian morality, unless they are prepared to take their stand upon the fundamentals of Christian theology. It is a lie to say that dogma does not matter; it matters enormously. It is fatal to let people suppose that Christianity is only a mode of feeling; it is vitally necessary to insist that it is first and foremost a rational explanation of the universe. It is hopeless to offer Christianity as a vaguely idealistic aspiration of a simple and consoling kind; it is, on the contrary, a hard, tough, exacting, and complex doctrine, steeped in a drastic and uncompromising realism. And it is fatal to imagine that everybody knows quite well what Christianity is and needs only a little encouragement to practise it. The brutal fact is that in this Christian country not one person in a hundred has the faintest notion what the Church teaches about God or man or society or the person of Jesus Christ. If you think I am exaggerating, ask the Army chaplains. Apart from a possible one per cent of intelligent and instructed Christians, there are three kinds of people we have to deal with. There are the frank and open heathen, whose notions of Christianity are a dreadful jumble of rags and tags of Bible anecdote and clotted mythological nonsense. There are the ignorant Christians, who combine a mild gentle-Jesus sentimentality with vaguely humanistic ethics—most of these are Arian heretics.* Finally, there are the more or less instructed church-goers, who know all the arguments about divorce and auricular confession and communion in two kinds, but are about as well equipped to do battle on fundamentals against a Marxian atheist or a Wellsian agnostic as a boy with a pea-shooter facing a fan-fire of machine-guns. Theologically, this country is at present in a state of utter chaos, established in the name of religious toleration, and rapidly degenerating into the flight from reason and the death of hope. We are not happy in this condition and there are signs of a very great eagerness, especially among the younger people, to find a creed to which they can give whole-hearted adherence.

This is the Church's opportunity, if she chooses to take it. So far as the people's readiness to listen goes, she has not been in so strong a position for at least two centuries. The rival philosophies of humanism, enlightened self-interest, and mechanical progress have broken down badly; the antagonism of science has proved to be far more apparent than real, and the happy-go-lucky doctrine of *laisser-faire* is completely discredited. But no good whatever will be done by a retreat into personal piety or by mere exhortation to a "recall to prayer." The thing that is in danger is the whole structure of society, and it is necessary to persuade thinking men and women of the vital and intimate connexion between the structure of society and the theological doctrines of Christianity.

The task is not made easier by the obstinate refusal of a great body of nominal Christians, both lay and clerical, to face the theological question. "Take away theology and give us some nice religion" has been a popular slogan for so long that we are apt to accept it, without inquiring whether religion without theology has any meaning. And however unpopular I may make myself I shall and will affirm that the reason why the Churches are discredited today is not that they are too bigoted about theology, but that they have

* Or possibly Adoptionists; they do not formulate their theories with any great precision.

run away from theology. The Church of Rome alone has retained her prestige because she puts theology in the foreground of her teaching. Some of us may perhaps think it a rather unimaginative and confined theology; but that is not the point. The point is that the Church of Rome is a theological society, in a sense in which the Church of England, taken as a whole, is not, and that because of this insistence on theology, she is a body disciplined, honoured, and sociologically important.

I should like to do two things this afternoon. First, to point out that if we really want a Christian society we must teach Christianity, and that it is absolutely impossible to teach Christianity without teaching Christian dogma. Secondly, to put before you a list of half a dozen or so main doctrinal points which the world most especially needs to have drummed into its ears at this moment—doctrines forgotten or misinterpreted, but which (if they are true as the Church maintains them to be) are corner-stones in that rational structure of human society which is the alternative to world-chaos.

I will begin with this matter of the inevitability of dogma, if Christianity is to be anything more than a little mild wishful-thinking about ethical behaviour.

Writing the other day in *The Spectator*, Dr. Selbie, former Principal of Mansfield College, discussed the subject of "The Army and the Churches." In the course of this article there occurs a passage that exposes the root-cause of the failure of the churches to influence the life of the common people.

". . . the rise of the new dogmatism (he says) whether in its Calvinist or Thomist form, constitutes a fresh and serious threat to Christian unity. The tragedy is that *all this, however interesting to theologians, is hopelessly irrelevant to the life and thought of the average man,* who is more puzzled than ever by the disunion of the Churches, and by the theological and ecclesiastical differences on which it is based."

Now I am perfectly ready to agree that disputes between the Churches constitute a menace to Christendom. And I will admit that I am not quite sure what is meant by "the new dogmatism"; it might, I suppose, mean the appearance of new dogmas among the followers of St. Thomas and Calvin respectively. But I rather fancy it means, a fresh attention to, and reassertion of, old dogma, and that when Dr. Selbie says that "all this" is irrelevant to the life and thought of the average man, he is deliberately saying that Christian dogma, as such, is irrelevant.

But if Christian dogma is irrelevant to life, to what, in Heaven's name is it relevant?—since religious dogma is in fact nothing but a statement of doctrines concerning the nature of life and the universe. If Christian ministers really believe it is only an intellectual game for theologians and has no bearing upon human life, it is no wonder that their congregations are ignorant, bored, and bewildered. And indeed, in the very next paragraph, Dr. Selbie recognizes the relation of Christian dogma to life:

> ". . . peace can only come about through a practical ap-
> plication of Christian principles and values. But this must have
> behind it *something more than a reaction against* that *Pagan
> Humanism* which has now been found wanting."

The "something else" is dogma, and cannot be anything else, for between Humanism and Christianity and between Paganism and Theism there is no distinction whatever except a distinction of dogma. That you cannot have Christian principles without Christ is becoming increasingly clear, because their validity as principles depends on Christ's authority; and as we have seen, the Totalitarian States, having ceased to believe in Christ's authority, are logically quite justified in repudiating Christian principles. If "the average man" is required to "believe in Christ" and accept His authority for "Christian principles," it is surely relevant to inquire who or what Christ is, and why His authority should be accepted. But the question, "What think ye of Christ?" lands the average man at once in the very knottiest kind of dogmatic riddle. It is quite useless to say that it doesn't matter particularly who or what Christ was or by what authority He did those things, and that even if He was only a man, He was a very nice man and we ought to live by His principles: for that is merely Humanism, and if the "average man" in Germany chooses to think that Hitler is a nicer sort of man with still more attractive principles, the Christian Humanist has no answer to make.

It is not true at all that dogma is "hopelessly irrelevant" to the life and thought of the average man. What is true is that ministers of the Christian religion often assert that it is, present it for consideration as though it were, and, in fact, by their faulty exposition of it make it so. The central dogma of the Incarnation is that by which relevance stands or falls. If Christ was only man, then He is entirely irrelevant to any thought about God; if He is only God, then He is entirely irrelevant to any experience of human life. It is, in the strictest sense, *necessary* to the salvation of relevance that a man should believe *rightly* the Incarnation of Our Lord Jesus Christ. Unless he believes rightly, there is not the faintest reason why he should believe at all. And in that case, it is wholly irrelevant to chatter about "Christian principles."

If the "average man" is going to be interested in Christ at all, it is the dogma that will provide the interest. The trouble is that, in nine cases out of ten, he has never been offered the dogma. What he has been offered is a set of technical theological terms which nobody has taken the trouble to translate into language relevant to ordinary life.

". . . Jesus Christ, the Son of God, is God and man." What does this suggest, except that God the Creator (the irritable old gentleman with the beard) in some mysterious manner fathered upon the Virgin Mary something amphibious, neither one thing nor t'other, like a merman? And, like human sons, wholly distinct from and (with some excuse) probably antagonistic to the father? And what, in any case, has this remarkable hybrid to do with John Brown or Tommy Atkins? This attitude of mind is that called by theologians Nestorianism, or perhaps a debased

form of Arianism. But we really cannot just give it a technical label and brush it aside as something irrelevant to
the thought of the average man. The average man produced it. It is, in fact, an immediate and unsophisticated
expression of the thought of the average man. And at the
risk of plunging him into the abominable heresy of the
Patripassians or the Theo-Paschites, we must unite with
Athanasius to assure Tommy Atkins that the God who
lived and died in the world was the same God who made
the world, and that, therefore, God Himself has the best
possible reasons for understanding and sympathizing with
Tommy's personal troubles.

"But," Tommy Atkins and John Brown will instantly
object, "it can't have mattered very much to Him if He was
God. A god can't really suffer like you and me. Besides,
the parson says we are to try and be like Christ; but that's
all nonsense—we can't be God, and it's silly to ask us to
try." This able exposition of the Eutychian heresy can
scarcely be dismissed as merely "interesting to theologians";
it appears to interest Atkins and Brown to the point of
irritation. Willy-nilly, we are forced to involve ourselves
further in dogmatic theology and insist that Christ is "perfect God *and perfect man.*"

At this point, language will trip us up. The average man
is not to be restrained from thinking that "perfect God"
implies a comparison with gods less perfect, and that "perfect man" means "the best kind of man you can possibly
have." While both these propositions are quite true, they
are not precisely what we want to convey. It will perhaps
be better to say, "altogether God and altogether man"—
God and man at the same time, in every respect and completely; God from eternity to eternity and from the womb
to the grave, a man also from the womb to the grave and
now.

"That," replies Tommy Atkins, "is all very well, but it
leaves me cold. Because, if He was God all the time He
must have known that His sufferings and death and so on
wouldn't last, and He could have stopped them by a miracle

if He had liked, so His pretending to be an ordinary man was nothing but play-acting." And John Brown adds, "You can't call a person 'altogether man' if He was God and didn't *want* to do anything wrong. It was easy enough for Him to be good, but it's not at all the same thing for me. How about all that temptation-stuff? Play-acting again. It doesn't help *me* to live what you call a Christian life."

John and Tommy are now on the way to become convinced Apollinarians, a fact which, however "interesting to theologians," has a distinct relevance also to the lives of those average men, since they propose, on the strength of it, to dismiss "Christian principles" as impracticable. There is no help for it. We must insist upon Christ's possession of "a reasonable soul" as well as "human flesh"; we must admit the human limitations of knowledge and intellect; we must take a hint from Christ Himself and suggest that miracles belong to the Son of Man as well as to the Son of God; we must postulate a human will liable to temptation; and we must be quite firm about "Equal to the Father as touching His Godhead *and inferior to the Father as touching His manhood.*" Complicated as the theology is, the average man has walked straight into the heart of the Athanasian Creed, and we are bound to follow.

Teachers and preachers never, I think, make it sufficiently clear that dogmas are not a set of arbitrary regulations invented *a priori* by a committee of theologians enjoying a bout of all-in dialectical wrestling. Most of them were hammered out under pressure of urgent practical necessity to provide an answer to heresy. And heresy is, as I have tried to show, largely the expression of opinion of the untutored average man, trying to grapple with the problems of the universe at the point where they begin to interfere with his daily life and thought. To me, engaged in my diabolical occupation of going to and fro in the world and walking up and down in it, conversations and correspondence bring daily a magnificent crop of all the standard heresies. As practical examples of the "life and thought of the average man" I am extremely well familiar with them, though I had to hunt through the Encyclopaedia to fit them with their proper theological titles for the purposes of this address. For the answers I need not go so far: they are compendiously set forth in the Creeds. But an interesting fact is this: that nine out of ten of my heretics are exceedingly surprised to discover that the Creeds contain any statements that bear a practical and comprehensible meaning. If I tell them it is an article of faith that the same God who made the world endured the suffering of the world, they ask in perfect good faith what connexion there is between that statement and the story of Jesus. If I draw their attention to the dogma that the same Jesus who was the Divine Love was also Light of Light, the Divine Wisdom, they are surprised. Some of them thank me very heartily for this entirely novel and original interpretation of Scripture, which they never heard of before and suppose me to have invented. Others say irritably that they don't like to think that wisdom and religion have anything to do with one another, and that I should do much better to cut out the wisdom and reason and intelligence and stick to a simple gospel of love. But whether they are pleased or annoyed, they are interested; and the thing that interests them, whether or not they suppose it to be my invention, is the resolute assertion of the dogma.

As regards Dr. Selbie's complaint that insistence on dogma only affronts people and throws into relief the internecine quarrels of Christendom, may I say two things? First, I believe it to be a grave mistake to present Christianity as something charming and popular with no offence in it. Seeing that Christ went about the world giving the most violent offence to all kinds of people it would seem absurd to expect that the doctrine of His Person can be so presented as to offend nobody. We cannot blink the fact that gentle Jesus meek and mild was so stiff in His opinions and so inflammatory in His language that He was thrown out of church, stoned, hunted from place to place, and finally gibbeted as a firebrand and a public danger. Whatever His peace was, it was not the peace of an amiable indifference; and He said in so many words that what He brought with Him was fire and sword. That being so, nobody need be too much surprised or disconcerted at finding that a determined preaching of Christian dogma may sometimes result in a few angry letters of protest or a difference of opinion on the parish council.

The other thing is this: that I find by experience there is a very large measure of agreement among Christian denominations on all doctrine that is really oecumenical. A rigidly Catholic interpretation of the Creeds, for example—including the Athanasian Creed—will find support both in Rome and in Geneva. Objections will come chiefly from the heathen, and from a noisy but not very representative bunch of heretical parsons who once in their youth read Robertson or Conybeare and have never got over it. But what is urgently necessary is that certain fundamentals should be restated in terms that make their meaning—and indeed, the mere fact that they *have* a meaning—clear to the ordinary uninstructed heathen to whom technical theological language has become a dead letter.

May I now mention some of the dogmas concerning which I find there is most ignorance and misunderstanding and about which I believe the modern world most urgently needs to be told? Out of a very considerable number I have selected seven as being what I may call "key-positions," namely, God, man, sin, judgment, matter, work, and society. They are, of course, all closely bound together—Christian doctrine is not a set of rules, but one vast interlocking rational structure—but there are particular aspects of these seven subjects which seem to me to need special emphasis at the moment.

1. GOD.—At the risk of appearing quite insolently obvious, I shall say that if the Church is to make any impression on the modern mind she will have to preach Christ and the cross.

Of late years, the Church has not succeeded very well in preaching Christ: she has preached Jesus, which is not quite the same thing. I find that the ordinary man simply does not grasp *at all* the idea that Jesus Christ and God the Creator are held to be literally the same person. They believe Catholic doctrine to be that God the Father made the world and that Jesus Christ redeemed mankind, and that these two characters are quite separate personalities. The phrasing of the Nicene Creed is here a little unfortunate—it is easy to read it as: "being of one substance with the-Father-by-whom-all-things-were-made." The Church Catechism—again rather unfortunately—emphasizes the distinction: "God the Father who hath made me and all the world, God the Son who hath redeemed me and all mankind." The distinction of the Persons within unity of the Substance is philosophically quite proper, and familiar enough to any creative artist: but the majority of people are not creative artists, and they have it very firmly fixed in their heads that the Person who bore the sins of the world was not the eternal creative life of the world, but an entirely different person, who was in fact the victim of God the Creator. It is dangerous to emphasize one aspect of a doctrine at the expense of the other, but at this present moment the danger that anybody will confound the Persons is so remote as to be negligible. What everybody does is to divide the substance—with the result that the whole Jesus-history becomes an unmeaning anecdote of the brutality of God to man.

It is only with the confident assertion of the creative divinity of the Son that the doctrine of the Incarnation becomes a real revelation of the structure of the world. And here Christianity has its enormous advantage over every other religion in the world. It is the *only* religion which gives value to evil and suffering. It affirms—not, like Christian Science, that evil has no real existence, nor yet, like Buddhism, that good consists in a refusal to experience evil—but that perfection is attained through the active and positive effort to wrench a real good out of a real evil.

I will not now go into the very difficult question of the nature of evil and the reality of not-being, though the modern physicists seem to be giving us a very valuable lead about that particular philosophic dilemma. But it seems to me most important that, in face of present world conditions, the doctrines of the reality of evil and the value of suffering should be kept in the very front line of Christian affirmation. I mean, it is not enough to say that religion produces virtues and personal consolations side by side with the very obvious evils and pains that afflict mankind, but that God is alive and at work *within* the evil and the suffering, perpetually transforming them by the positive energy which He had with the Father before the world was made.

2. MAN.—A young and intelligent priest remarked to me the other day that he thought one of the greatest sources of strength in Christianity today lay in the profoundly pessimistic view it took of human nature. There is a great deal in what he says. The people who are most discouraged and made despondent by the barbarity and stupidity of human behaviour at this time are those who think highly of *Homo Sapiens* as a product of evolution, and who still cling to an optimistic belief in the civilizing influence of progress and enlightenment. To them, the appalling outbursts of bestial ferocity in the Totalitarian States, and the obstinate selfishness and stupid greed of Capitalist Society, are not merely shocking and alarming. For them, these things are the utter negation of everything in which they have believed. It is as though the bottom had dropped out of their universe. The whole thing looks like a denial of all reason, and they feel as if they and the world had gone mad together. Now for the Christian, this is not so. He is as deeply shocked and grieved as anybody else, but he is not astonished. He has never thought very highly of human nature left to itself. He has been accustomed to the idea that there is a deep interior dislocation in the very centre of human personality, and that you can never, as they say, "make people good by Act of Parliament," just because laws are man-made and therefore partake of the imperfect and self-contradictory nature of man. Humanly speaking, it is not true at all that "truly to know the good is to do the good"; it is far truer to

say with St. Paul that "the evil that I would not, that I do"; so that the mere increase of knowledge is of very little help in the struggle to outlaw evil. The delusion of the mechanical perfectibility of mankind through a combined process of scientific knowledge and unconscious evolution has been responsible for a great deal of heartbreak. It is, at bottom, far more pessimistic than Christian pessimism, because, if science and progress break down, there is nothing to fall back upon. Humanism is self-contained—it provides for man no resources outside himself. The Christian dogma of the double nature in man—which asserts that man is disintegrated and necessarily imperfect is himself and all his works, yet closely related by a real unity of substance with an eternal perfection within and beyond him—makes the present parlous state of human society seem both less hopeless and less irrational. I say "the present parlous state"—but that is to limit it too much. A man told me the other day: "I have a little boy of a year old. When the war broke out, I was very much distressed about him, because I found I was taking it for granted that life *ought* to be better and easier for him than it had been for my generation. Then I realized that I had no right to take this for granted at all— that the fight between good and evil must be the same for him as it had always been, and then I ceased to feel so much distressed." As Lord David Cecil has said: "The jargon of the philosophy of progress taught us to think that the savage and primitive state of man is behind us; we still talk of the present 'return to barbarism.' But barbarism is not behind us, it is beneath us." And in the same article he observes: "Christianity has compelled the mind of man, not because it is the most cheering view of human existence, but because it is truest to the facts." I think this is true; and it seems to me quite disastrous that the idea should have got about that Christianity is an other-worldly, unreal, idealistic kind of religion which suggests that if we are good we shall be happy—or if not, it will all be made up to us in the next existence. On the contrary, it is fiercely and even harshly realistic, insisting that the Kingdom of

Heaven can never be attained in this world except by un-
ceasing toil and struggle and vigilance: that, in fact, we
cannot be good and cannot be happy, but that there are
certain eternal achievements that make even happiness look
like trash. It has been said, I think by Berdyaev, that nothing can prevent the human soul from preferring creativeness to happiness. In this lies man's substantial likeness to
the Divine Christ who in this world suffers and creates continually, being incarnate in the bonds of matter.

3. SIN.—This doctrine of man leads naturally to the doctrine of sin. One of the really surprising things about
the present bewilderment of humanity is that the Christian
Church now finds herself called upon to proclaim the old
and hated doctrine of sin as a gospel of cheer and encouragement. The final tendency of the modern philosophies—
hailed in their day as a release from the burden of sinfulness—has been to bind man hard and fast in the chains of
an iron determinism. The influences of heredity and en-
vironment, of glandular make-up and the control exercised
by the unconscious, of economic necessity and the mechan-
ics of biological development, have all been invoked to
assure man that he is not responsible for his misfortunes
and therefore not to be held guilty. Evil has been represented as something imposed upon him from without, not
made by him from within. The dreadful conclusion follows inevitably, that as he is not responsible for evil, he
cannot alter it; even though evolution and progress may
offer some alleviation in the future, there is no hope for
you and me, here and now. I well remember how an aunt
of mine, brought up in an old-fashioned liberalism, protested angrily against having continually to call herself a
"miserable sinner" when reciting the Litany. Today, if we
could really be persuaded that we *are* miserable sinners—
that the trouble is not outside us but inside us, and that
therefore, by the grace of God we can do something to
put it right, we should receive that message as the most
hopeful and heartening thing that can be imagined.

Needless to say, the whole doctrine of "original sin" will

have to be restated, in terms which the ordinary modern man, brought up on biology and Freudian psychology, can understand. These sciences have done an enormous amount to expose the *nature* and *mechanism* of man's inner dislocation and ought to be powerful weapons in the hand of the Church. It is a thousand pities that the Church should ever have allowed these weapons to be turned against her.

4. JUDGMENT.—Much the same thing is true of the doctrine of judgment. The word "punishment" for sin has become so corrupted that it ought never to be used. But once we have established the true doctrine of man's nature, the true nature of judgment becomes startlingly clear and rational. It is the inevitable consequence of man's attempt to regulate life and society on a system that runs counter to the facts of his own nature. In the physical sphere, typhus and cholera are a judgment on dirty living; not because God shows an arbitrary favouritism to nice, clean people, but because of an essential element in the physical structure of the universe. In the state, the brutal denial of freedom to the individual will issue in a judgment of blood, because man is so made that oppression is more intolerable to him than death. The avaricious greed that prompts men to cut down forests for the speedy making of money brings down a judgment of flood and famine, because that sin of avarice in the spiritual sphere runs counter to the physical law of nature. We must not say that such behaviour is wrong because it does not pay; but rather that it does not pay because it is wrong. As T. S. Eliot says: "A wrong attitude towards nature implies, somewhere, a wrong attitude towards God, and the consequence is an inevitable doom."

5. MATTER.—At this point we shall find ourselves compelled to lay down the Christian doctrine concerning the material universe; and it is here, I think, that we shall have our best opportunity to explain the meaning of sacramentalism. The common man labours under a delusion that for the Christian, matter is evil and the body is evil. For this misapprehension, St. Paul must bear some blame, St.

Augustine of Hippo a good deal more, and Calvin a very
great deal. But so long as the Church continues to teach
the manhood of God and to celebrate the sacraments of
the Eucharist and of marriage, no living man should dare
to say that matter and body are not sacred to her. She must
insist strongly that the whole material universe is an expression and incarnation of the creative energy of God, as
a book or a picture is the material expression of the creative soul of the artist. For that reason, all good and creative
handling of the material universe is holy and beautiful,
and all abuse of the material universe is a crucifixion of the
body of Christ. The whole question of the right use to be
made of art, of the intellect, and of the material resources
of the world is bound up in this. Because of this, the exploitation of man or of matter for commercial uses stands condemned, together with all debasement of the arts and per-
versions of the intellect. If matter and the physical nature
of man are evil, or if they are of no importance except as
they serve an economic system, then there is nothing to
restrain us from abusing them as we choose—nothing, except the absolute certainty that any such abuse will even-
tually come up against the unalterable law and issue in
judgment and destruction. In these as in all other matters
we cannot escape the law; we have only the choice of fulfilling it freely by the way of grace or willy-nilly by the way
of judgment.

6. WORK.—The unsacramental attitude of modern society
to man and matter is probably closely connected with its
unsacramental attitude to work. The Church is a good deal
to blame for having connived at this. From the eighteenth
century onwards, she has tended to acquiesce in what I may
call the "industrious apprentice" view of the matter:
"Work hard and be thrifty, and God will bless you with
a contented mind and a competence." This is nothing but
enlightened self-interest in its vulgarest form, and plays
directly into the hands of the monopolist and the financier.
Nothing has so deeply discredited the Christian Church as
her squalid submission to the economic theory of society.

The burning question of the Christian attitude to money is being so eagerly debated nowadays that it is scarcely necessary to do more than remind ourselves that the present unrest, both in Russia and in Central Europe, is an immediate judgment upon a financial system that has subordinated man to economics, and that no *mere* readjustment of economic machinery will have any lasting effect if it keeps man a prisoner inside the machine.

This is the burning question; but I believe there is a still more important and fundamental question waiting to be dealt with, and that is, what men in a Christian Society ought to think and feel about work. Curiously enough, apart from the passage in *Genesis* which suggests that work is a hardship and a judgment on sin, Christian doctrine is not very explicit about work. I believe, however, that there *is* a Christian doctrine of work, very closely related to the doctrines of the creative energy of God and the divine image in man. The modern tendency seems to be to identify work with gainful employment; and this is, I maintain, the essential heresy at the back of the great economic fallacy which allows wheat and coffee to be burnt and fish to be used for manure while whole populations stand in need of food. The fallacy being that work is not the expression of man's creative energy in the service of Society, but only something he does in order to obtain money and leisure.

A very able surgeon put it to me like this: "What is happening," he said, "is that nobody works for the sake of getting the thing done. The result of the work is a by-product; the *aim* of the work is to make money to do something else. Doctors practise medicine, not primarily to relieve suffering, but to make a living—the cure of the patient is something that happens on the way. Lawyers accept briefs, not because they have a passion for justice, but because the law is the profession which enables them to live. The reason," he added, "why men often find themselves happy and satisfied in the army is that for the first time in their lives they find themselves doing something, not for the sake of the pay, which is miserable, but for the sake of getting the thing done."

I will only add to this one thing which seems to me very symptomatic. I was shown a "scheme for a Christian Society" drawn up by a number of young and earnest Roman Catholics. It contained a number of clauses dealing with work and employment—minimum wages, hours of labour, treatment of employees, housing, and so on—all very proper and Christian. But it offered no machinery whatever for ensuring that the work itself should be properly done. In its lack of a sacramental attitude to work, that is, it was as empty as a set of trade union regulations. We may remember that a medieval guild did insist, not only on the employer's duty to his workmen, but also on the labourer's duty to his work.

If man's fulfilment of his nature is to be found in the full expression of his divine creativeness, then we urgently need a Christian doctrine of work, which shall provide, not only for proper conditions of employment, but also that the work shall be such as a man may do with his whole heart, and that he shall do it for the very work's sake. But we cannot expect a sacramental attitude to work, while many people are forced, by our evil standard of values, to do work which is a spiritual degradation—a long series of financial trickeries, for example, or the manufacture of vulgar and useless trivialities.

7. SOCIETY.—Lastly, a word or two about the Christian doctrine of society—not about its translation into political terms, but about its dogmatic basis. It rests on the doctrine of what God is and what man is, and it is impossible to have a Christian doctrine of society *except* as a corollary to Christian dogma about the place of man in the universe. This is, or should be, obvious. The one point to which I should like to draw attention is the Christian doctrine of the moral law. The attempt to abolish wars and wickedness by the moral law is doomed to failure, because of the fact of sinfulness. Law, like every other product of human activity, shares the integral human imperfection:

it is, in the old Calvinistic phrase: "of the nature of sin." That is to say: all legality, if erected into an absolute value, contains within itself the seeds of judgment and catastrophe. The law is necessary, but only, as it were, as a protective fence against the forces of evil, behind which the divine activity of grace may do its redeeming work. We can, for example, never make a positive peace or a positive righteousness by enactments against offenders; law is always prohibitive, negative, and corrupted by the interior contradictions of man's divided nature; it belongs to the category of judgment. That is why an intelligent understanding about sin is necessary to preserve the world from putting an unjustified confidence in the efficacy of the moral law taken by itself. It will never drive out Beelzebub; it cannot, because it is only human and not divine.

Nevertheless, the law must be rightly understood or it is not possible to make the world understand the meaning of grace. There is only one real law—the law of the universe; it may be fulfilled either by way of judgment or by the way of grace, but it *must* be fulfilled one way or the other. If men will not understand the meaning of judgment, they will never come to understand the meaning of grace. If they hear not Moses or the Prophets, neither will they be persuaded, though one rose from the dead.

VI. Why Work? *

I HAVE already, on a previous occasion,† spoken at some
length on the subject of Work and Vocation. What I urged
then was a thorough-going revolution in our whole attitude
to work. I asked that it should be looked upon—not as a
necessary drudgery to be undergone for the purpose of
making money, but as a way of life in which the nature of
man should find its proper exercise and delight and so ful-
fil itself to the glory of God. That it should, in fact, be
thought of as a creative activity undertaken for the love
of the work itself; and that man, made in God's image,
should make things, as God makes them, for the sake of
doing well a thing that is well worth doing.

It may well seem to you—as it does to some of my ac-
quaintances—that I have a sort of obsession about this business of the right attitude to work. But I do insist upon
it, because it seems to me that what becomes of civilization after this war is going to depend enormously on our
being able to effect this revolution in our ideas about work.
Unless we do change our whole way of thought about work,
I do not think we shall ever escape from the appalling
squirrel-cage of economic confusion in which we have been
madly turning for the last three centuries or so, the cage
in which we landed ourselves by acquiescing in a social
system based upon Envy and Avarice. A society in which
consumption has to be artificially stimulated in order to
keep production going is a society founded on trash and
waste, and such a society is a house built upon sand.

It is interesting to consider for a moment how our outlook has been forcibly changed for us in the last twelve

* An address delivered at Eastbourne, England, April 23, 1942.
† At Brighton, March 1941. The major part of the address was
printed in *A Christian Basis for the Post-War World* (S.C.M. Press).

months by the brutal presence of war. War is a judgment
that overtakes societies when they have been living upon
ideas that conflict too violently with the laws governing
the universe. People who would not revise their ideas voluntarily find themselves compelled to do so by the sheer
pressure of the events which these very ideas have served
to bring about. Never think that wars are irrational catas-
trophes: they happen when wrong ways of thinking and
living bring about intolerable situations; and whichever
side may be the more outrageous in its aims and the more
brutal in its methods, the root causes of conflict are usually
to be found in some wrong way of life in which all parties
have acquiesced, and for which everybody must, to some
extent, bear the blame. It is quite true that false Economics are one of the root causes of the present war; and one
of the false ideas we had about Economics was a false attitude both to Work and to the goods produced by Work.
This attitude we are now being obliged to alter, under the
compulsion of war—and a very strange and painful process
it is in some ways. It is always strange and painful to have
to change a habit of mind; though, when we have made
the effort, we may find a great relief, even a sense of adventure and delight, in getting rid of the false and return-
ing to the true.

Can you remember—it is already getting difficult to remember—what things were like before the war? The stockings we bought cheap and threw away to save the trouble
of mending? The cars we scrapped every year to keep up
with the latest fashion in engine-design and streamlining?
The bread and bones and scraps of fat that littered the
dustbins—not only of the rich, but of the poor? The empty
bottles that even the dustman scorned to collect, because
the manufacturers found it cheaper to make new ones than
to clean the old? The mountains of empty tins that nobody
found it worth while to salvage, rusting and stinking on
the refuse-dumps? The food that was burnt or buried because it did not pay to distribute it? The land choked and
impoverished with thistle and ragwort, because it did not

pay to farm it? The handkerchiefs used for paint-rags and kettle-holders? The electric lights left blazing because it was too much trouble to switch them off? The fresh peas we could not be bothered to shell, and threw aside for something out of a tin? The paper that cumbered the shelves, and lay knee-deep in the parks, and littered the seats of railway-trains? The scattered hairpins and smashed crockery, the trumpery knick-knacks of steel and wood and rubber and glass and tin that we bought to fill in an odd half-hour at Woolworth's and forgot as soon as we had bought them? The advertisements imploring and exhorting and cajoling and menacing and bullying us to glut ourselves with things we did not want, in the name of snobbery and idleness and sex-appeal? And the fierce international scramble to find in helpless and backward nations a market on which to fob off all the superfluous rubbish which the inexorable machines ground out hour by hour, to create money and to create employment? Do you realize how we have had to alter our whole scale of values, now that we are no longer being urged to consume but to conserve? We have been forced back to the social morals of our great-grandparents. When a piece of lingerie costs three precious coupons, we have to consider, not merely its glamour-value, but how long it will wear. When fats are rationed, we must not throw away scraps, but jealously use to advantage what it cost so much time and trouble to breed and rear. When paper is scarce we must—or we should—think whether what we have to say is worth saying before writing or printing it. When our life depends on the land, we have to pay in short commons for destroying its fertility by neglect or over-cropping. When a haul of herrings takes valuable manpower from the forces, and is gathered in at the peril of men's lives by bomb and mine and machine-gun, we read a new significance into those gloomy words which appear so often in the fishmonger's shop: NO FISH TODAY. . . . We have had to learn the bitter lesson that in all the world there are only two sources of real wealth: the fruit of the earth and the labour of men; and to estimate work—not by the money it brings to the producer, but by the worth of the thing that is made.

The question that I will ask you to consider today is this: When the war is over, are we likely, and *do we want* to keep this attitude to work and the results of work? or are we preparing and *do we want,* to go back to our old habits of thought? Because I believe that on our answer to this question the whole economic future of society will depend. Sooner or later the moment will come when we have to make a decision about this. At the moment, we are not making it—don't let us flatter ourselves that we are. It is being made for us. And don't let us imagine that a war-time economy has stopped waste. It has not. It has only transferred it elsewhere. The glut and waste that used to clutter our own dustbins have been removed to the field of battle. That is where all the surplus consumption is going to. The factories are roaring more loudly than ever, turning out night and day goods that are of no conceivable value for the maintenance of life; on the contrary, their sole object is to destroy life, and instead of being thrown away they are being blown away—in Russia, in North Africa, over Occupied France, in Burma and China, and the Spice Islands, and on the Seven Seas. What is going to happen when the factories stop turning out armaments? No nation has yet found a way to keep the machines running and whole nations employed under modern industrial conditions without wasteful consumption. For a time, a few nations could contrive to keep going by securing a monopoly of production and forcing their waste products on to new and untapped markets. When there are no new markets and all nations are industrial producers, the only choice we have been able to envisage so far has been that between armaments and unemployment. This is the problem that some time or other will stare us in the face again, and this time we must have our minds ready to tackle it. It may not come at once—for it is quite likely that after the war we shall have to go through a further period of managed consumption while the shortages caused by the

war are being made good. But sooner or later we shall have
to grapple with this difficulty, and everything will depend
on our attitude of mind about it. Shall we be prepared
to take the same attitude to the arts of peace as to the arts
of war? I see no reason why we should not sacrifice our
convenience and our individual standard of living just as
readily for the building of great public works as for the
building of ships and tanks—but when the stimulus of fear
and anger is removed, shall we be prepared to do any such
thing? Or shall we *want* to go back to that civilization of
greed and waste which we dignify by the name of a "high
standard of living"? I am getting very much afraid of that
phrase about the standard of living. And I am also frightened by the phrase "after the war"—it is so often pro-
nounced in a tone that suggests: "after the war, we want to
relax, and go back, and live as we did before." And that
means going back to the time when labour was valued in
terms of its cash returns, and not in terms of the work.

Now the answer to this question, if we are resolute to
know what we are about, will not be left to rich men—to
manufacturers and financiers. If these people have governed the world of late years it is only because we ourselves
put the power into their hands. The question can and
should be answered by the worker and the consumer. It is
extremely important that the worker should really understand where the problem lies. It is a matter of brutal fact
that in these days labour, more than any other section of
the community, has a vested interest in war. Some rich employers make profit out of war—that is true; but what is
infinitely more important is that for all working people
war means full employment and high wages. When war
ceases, then the problem of employing labour at the machines begins again. The relentless pressure of hungry labour is behind the drive toward wasteful consumption,
whether in the destruction of war or in the trumpery of
peace. The problem is far too much simplified when it is
presented as a mere conflict between labour and capital,
between employed and employer. The basic difficulty re-

mains, even when you make the State the sole employer,
even when you make Labour into the employer. It is not
simply a question of profits and wages or living conditions
—but of what is to be done with the work of the machines,
and what work the machines are to do. If we do not deal
with this question now, while we have time to think about
it, then the whirligig of wasteful production and wasteful
consumption will start again and will again end in war.
And the driving-power of labour will be thrusting to turn
the wheels, because it is to the financial interest of labour
to keep the whirligig going faster and faster till the inevitable catastrophe comes.

And, so that the wheels may turn, the consumer—that is,
you and I, including the workers, who are consumers also—
will again be urged to consume and waste; and unless we
change our attitude—or rather unless we keep hold of the
new attitude forced upon us by the logic of war—we shall
again be bamboozled by our vanity, indolence, and greed
into keeping the squirrel-cage of wasteful economy turning.
We could—you and I—bring the whole fantastic economy
of profitable waste down to the ground overnight, without
legislation and without revolution, merely by refusing to
co-operate with it. I say, we could—as a matter of fact, we
have; or rather, it has been done for us. If we do not want
it to rise up again after the war, we can prevent it—simply
by preserving the war-time habit of valuing work instead
of money. The point is: do we *want* to? . . . Whatever we
do, we shall be faced with grave difficulties. That cannot
be disguised. But it will make a great difference to the
result if we are genuinely aiming at a real change in economic thinking. And by that I mean a radical change from
top to bottom—a new system; not a mere adjustment of the
old system to favour a different set of people. The habit
of thinking about work as something one does to make
money is so ingrained in us that we can scarcely imagine
what a revolutionary change it would be to think about it
instead in terms of the work done. It would mean taking
the attitude of mind we reserve for our unpaid work—

our hobbies, our leisure interests, the things we make and do for pleasure—and making *that* the standard of all our judgments about things and people. We should ask of an enterprise, not "will it pay?" but "is it good?"; of a man, not "what does he make?" but "what is his work worth?"; of goods, not "can we induce people to buy them?" but "are they useful things well made?"; of employment, not "how much a week?" but "will it exercise my faculties to the utmost?" And shareholders in—let us say—brewing companies, would astonish the directorate by arising at shareholders' meetings and demanding to know, not merely where the profits go or what dividends are to be paid, not even merely whether the workers' wages are sufficient and the conditions of labour satisfactory, but loudly, and with a proper sense of personal responsibility: What goes into the beer?

You will probably ask at once: How is this altered attitude going to make any difference to the question of employment? Because it sounds as though it would result in not more employment, but less. I am not an economist, and I can only point to a peculiarity of war economy that usually goes without notice in economic text-books. In war, production for wasteful consumption still goes on: but there is one great difference in the goods produced. None of them is valued for what it will fetch, but only for what it is worth in itself. The gun and the tank, the aeroplane and the warship have to be the best of their kind. A war consumer does not buy shoddy. He does not buy to sell again. He buys the thing that is good for its purpose, asking nothing of it but that it shall do the job it has to do. Once again, war forces the consumer into a right attitude to the work. And, whether by strange coincidence, or whether because of some universal law, so soon as nothing is demanded of the thing made but its own integral perfection, its own absolute value, the skill and labour of the worker are fully employed and likewise acquire an absolute value.

This is probably not the kind of answer that you will

find in any theory of economics. But the professional economist is not really trained to answer, or even to ask himself
questions about absolute values. The economist is inside
the squirrel-cage and turning with it. Any question about
absolute values belongs to the sphere, not of economics,
but of religion. And it is very possible that we cannot deal
with economics at all, unless we can see economy from outside the cage; that we cannot begin to settle the relative
values without considering absolute values. And if so, this
may give a very precise and practical meaning to the words:
"Seek first the kingdom of God and righteousness, and all
these things shall be added to you." . . . I am persuaded
that the reason why the Churches are in so much difficulty
about giving a lead in the economic sphere is because they
are trying to fit a Christian standard of economics to a
wholly false and pagan understanding of work.

What is the Christian understanding of work? . . . I
should like to put before you two or three propositions
arising out of the doctrinal position which I stated at the
beginning: namely, that work is the natural exercise and
function of man—the creature who is made in the image of
his Creator. You will find that any one of them, if given in
effect everyday practice, is so revolutionary (as compared
with the habits of thinking into which we have fallen), as
to make all political revolutions look like conformity.

The first, stated quite briefly, is that work is not, primarily, a thing one does to live, but the thing one lives to
do. It is, or it should be, the full expression of the worker's
faculties, the thing in which he finds spiritual, mental, and
bodily satisfaction, and the medium in which he offers
himself to God.

Now the consequences of this are not merely that the
work should be performed under decent living and working conditions. That is a point we have begun to grasp, and
it is a perfectly sound point. But we have tended to con-
centrate on it to the exclusion of other considerations far
more revolutionary.

(*a*) There is, for instance, the question of profits and

remuneration. We have all got it fixed in our heads that the proper end of work is to be paid for—to produce a return in profits or payment to the worker which fully or more than compensates the effort he puts into it. But if our proposition is true, this does not follow at all. So long as Society provides the worker with a sufficient return in real wealth to enable him to carry on the work properly, then he has his reward. For his work is the measure of his life, and his satisfaction is found in the fulfilment of his own nature, and in contemplation of the perfection of his work. That, in practice, there is this satisfaction, is shown by the mere fact that a man will put loving labour into some hobby which can never bring him in any economically adequate return. His satisfaction comes, in the god-like manner, from looking upon what he has made and finding it very good. He is no longer bargaining with his work, but serving it. It is only when work has to be looked on as a means to gain that it becomes hateful; for then, instead of a friend, it becomes an enemy from whom tolls and contributions have to be extracted. What most of us demand from society is that we should always get out of it a little *more* than the value of the labour we give to it. By this process, we persuade ourselves that society is always in our debt—a conviction that not only piles up actual financial burdens, but leaves us with a grudge against society.

(b) Here is the second consequence. At present we have no clear grasp of the principle that every man should do the work for which he is fitted by nature. The employer is obsessed by the notion that he must find cheap labour, and the worker by the notion that the best-paid job is the job for him. Only feebly, inadequately, and spasmodically do we ever attempt to tackle the problem from the other end, and inquire: What type of worker is suited to this type of work? People engaged in education see clearly that this *is* the right end to start from; but they are frustrated by economic pressure, and by the failure of parents on the one hand and employers on the other to grasp the fundamental importance of this approach. And that the trouble results far more from a failure of intelligence than from economic necessity is seen clearly under war conditions, when, though competitive economics are no longer a governing factor, the right men and women are still persistently thrust into the wrong jobs, through sheer inability on everybody's part to imagine a purely vocational approach to the business of fitting together the worker and his work.

(c) A third consequence is that, if we really believed this proposition and arranged our work and our standard of values accordingly, we should no longer think of work as something that we hastened to get through in order to enjoy our leisure; we should look on our leisure as the period of changed rhythm that refreshed us for the delightful purpose of getting on with our work. And, this being so, we should tolerate no regulations of any sort that prevented us from working as long and as well as our enjoyment of work demanded. We should resent any such restrictions as a monstrous interference with the liberty of the subject. How great an upheaval of our ideas that would mean I leave you to imagine. It would turn topsy-turvy all our notions about hours of work, rates of work, unfair competition, and all the rest of it. We should all find ourselves fighting, as now only artists and the members of certain professions fight, for precious time in which to get on with the job—instead of fighting for precious hours saved from the job.

(d) A fourth consequence is that we should fight tooth and nail, not for mere employment, but for the quality of the work that we had to do. We should clamour to be engaged on work that was worth doing, and in which we could take a pride. The worker would demand that the stuff he helped to turn out should be good stuff—he would no longer be content to take the cash and let the credit go. Like the shareholders in the brewery, he would feel a sense of personal responsibility, and clamour to know, and to control, what went into the beer he brewed. There would be protests and strikes—not only about pay and conditions, but about the quality of the work demanded and the honesty, beauty, and usefulness of the goods produced. The greatest insult which a commercial age has offered to the worker has been to rob him of all interest in the end-product of the work and to force him to dedicate his life to making badly things which were not worth making.

This first proposition chiefly concerns the worker as such. My second proposition directly concerns Christians as such, and it is this: It is the business of the Church to recognize that the secular vocation, as such, is sacred. Christian people, and particularly perhaps the Christian clergy, must get it firmly into their heads that when a man or woman is called to a particular job of secular work, that is as true a vocation as though he or she were called to specifically religious work. The Church must concern herself not only with such questions as the just price and proper working conditions: she must concern herself with seeing that the work itself is such as a human being can perform without degradation—that no one is required by economic or any other considerations to devote himself to work that is contemptible, soul-destroying, or harmful. It is not right for her to acquiesce in the notion that a man's life is divided into the time he spends on his work and the time he spends in serving God. He must be able to serve God *in* his work, and the work itself must be accepted and respected as the medium of divine creation.

In nothing has the Church so lost her hold on reality as in her failure to understand and respect the secular vocation. She has allowed work and religion to become separate departments, and is astonished to find that, as a result, the secular work of the world is turned to purely selfish and destructive ends, and that the greater part of the world's intelligent workers have become irreligious, or at least, uninterested in religion. But is it astonishing? How can any one remain interested in a religion which seems to have no concern with nine-tenths of his life? The Church's approach to an intelligent carpenter is usually confined to exhorting him not to be drunk and disorderly in his leisure hours, and to come to church on Sundays. What the Church *should* be telling him is this: that the very first demand that his religion makes upon him is that he should make good tables. Church by all means, and decent forms of amusement, certainly—but what use is all that if in the very centre of his life and occupation he is insulting God with bad carpentry? No crooked table-legs or ill-fitting drawers ever, I dare swear, came out of the carpenter's shop at Nazareth. Nor, if they did, could anyone believe that they were made by the same hand that made heaven and earth. No piety in the worker will compensate for work that is not true to itself; for any work that is untrue to its own technique is a living lie. Yet in her own buildings, in her own ecclesiastical art and music, in her hymns and prayers, in her sermons and in her little books of devotion, the Church will tolerate, or permit a pious intention to excuse, work so ugly, so pretentious, so tawdry and twaddling, so insincere and insipid, so *bad* as to shock and horrify any decent draftsman. And why? Simply because she has lost all sense of the fact that the living and eternal truth is expressed in work only so far as that work is true in itself, to itself, to the standards of its own technique. She has forgotten that the secular vocation is sacred. Forgotten that a building must be good architecture before it can be a good church; that a painting must be well painted before it can be a good sacred picture; that work must be good work before it can call itself God's work.

Let the Church remember this: that every maker and worker is called to serve God *in* his profession or trade—not outside it. The Apostles complained rightly when they said it was not meet they should leave the word of God and serve tables; their vocation was to preach the word. But the person whose vocation it is to prepare the meals beautifully might with equal justice protest: It is not meet for us to leave the service of our tables to preach the word. The official Church wastes time and energy, and, moreover, commits sacrilege, in demanding that secular workers should

neglect their proper vocation in order to do Christian
work—by which she means ecclesiastical work. The only
Christian work is good work well done. Let the Church
see to it that the workers are Christian people and do their
work well, as to God: then all the work will be Christian
work, whether it is Church embroidery, or sewage-farming.
As Jacques Maritain says: "If you want to produce Christian work, be a Christian, and try to make a work of beauty
into which you have put your heart; do not adopt a Christian pose." He is right. And let the Church remember that
the beauty of the work will be judged by its own, and not
by ecclesiastical standards. Let me give you an illustration
of what I mean. When my play *The Zeal of Thy House*
was produced in London, a dear old pious lady was much
struck by the beauty of the four great archangels who stood
throughout the play in their heavy, gold robes, eleven feet
high from wing-tip to sandal-tip. She asked with great innocence "whether I selected the actors who played the angels
for the excellence of their moral character?" I replied that
the angels were selected, to begin with, not by me but by
the producer, who had the technical qualifications for
selecting suitable actors—for that was part of his vocation.
And that he selected, in the first place, young men who
were six feet tall, so that they would match properly together. Secondly, angels had to be of good physique, so as
to be able to stand stiff on the stage for two and a half
hours, carrying the weight of their wings and costumes,
without wobbling, or fidgeting, or fainting. Thirdly, they
must be able to speak verse well, in an agreeable voice and
audibly. Fourthly, they must be reasonably good actors.
When all these technical conditions were fulfilled, we
might come to the moral qualities, of which the first would
be the ability to arrive on the stage punctually and in a
sober condition, since the curtain must go up on time, and
a drunken angel would be indecorous. After that, and only
after that, one might take character into consideration, but
that—provided his behaviour was not so scandalous as to
cause dissension among the company—the right kind of

actor with no morals would give a far more reverent and seemly performance than a saintly actor with the wrong technical qualifications. The worst religious films I ever saw were produced by a company which chose its staff exclusively for their piety. Bad photography, bad acting, and bad dialogue produced a result so grotesquely irreverent that the pictures could not have been shown in churches without bringing Christianity into contempt. God is not served by technical incompetence; and incompetence and untruth always result when the secular vocation is treated as a thing alien to religion. . . . And conversely: when you find a man who is a Christian praising God by the excellence of his work—do not distract him and take him away from his proper vocation to address religious meetings and open church bazaars. Let him serve God in the way to which God has called him. If you take him away from that, he will exhaust himself in an alien technique and lose his capacity to do his dedicated work. It is your business, you churchmen, to get what good you can from observing his work—not to take him away from it, so that he may do ecclesiastical work for you. But, if you have any power, see that he is set free to do his own work as well as it may be done. He is not there to serve you; he is there to serve God by serving his work.

This brings me to my third proposition; and this may sound to you the most revolutionary of all. It is this: the worker's first duty is to *serve the work*. The popular "catch" phrase of today is that it is everybody's duty to serve the community. It is a well-sounding phrase, but there *is* a catch in it. It is the old catch about the two great commandments. "Love God—and your neighbour; on those two commandments hang all the Law and the Prophets." The catch in it, which nowadays the world has largely forgotten, is that the second commandment depends upon the first, and that without the first, it is a delusion and a snare. Much of our present trouble and disillusionment have come from putting the second commandment before the first. If we put our neighbour first,

we are putting man above God, and that is what we have
been doing ever since we began to worship humanity and
make man the measure of all things. Whenever man is
made the centre of things, he becomes the storm-centre of
trouble—and that is precisely the catch about serving the
community. It ought perhaps to make us suspicious of that
phrase when we consider that it is the slogan of every commercial scoundrel and swindler who wants to make sharp
business practice pass muster as social improvement. "Service" is the motto of the advertiser, of big business, and of
fraudulent finance. And of others, too. Listen to this: "I
expect the judicature to understand that the nation does
not exist for their convenience, but that justice exists to
serve the nation." That was Hitler yesterday—and that is
what becomes of "service," when the community, and not
the work, becomes its idol. There is, in fact, a paradox
about working to serve the community, and it is this: that
to aim directly at serving the community is to falsify the
work; the only way to serve the community is to forget
the community and serve the work. There are three very
good reasons for this:

The first is, that you cannot do good work if you take
your mind off the work to see how the community is taking
it—any more than you can make a good drive from the tee
if you take your eye off the ball. "Blessed are the single-
hearted" (for that is the real meaning of the word we translate *"the pure in heart"*). If your heart is not wholly in the
work, the work will not be good—and work that is not good
serves neither God nor the community; it only serves Mammon.

The second reason is that the moment you think of serving other people, you begin to have a notion that other
people owe you something for your pains; you begin to
think that you have a claim on the community. You will
begin to bargain for reward, to angle for applause, and to
harbour a grievance if you are not appreciated. But if your
mind is set upon serving the work, then you know you have
nothing to look for; the only reward the *work* can give you

is the satisfaction of beholding its perfection. The work takes all and gives nothing but itself; and to serve the work is a labour of pure love.

And thirdly, if you set out to serve the community, you will probably end by merely fulfilling a public demand—and you may not even do that. A public demand is a changeable thing. Nine-tenths of the bad plays put on in theatres owe their badness to the fact that the playwright has aimed at pleasing the audience, instead of at producing a good and satisfactory play. Instead of doing the work as its own integrity demands that it should be done, he has falsified the play by putting in this or that which he thinks will appeal to the groundlings (who by that time have probably come to want something else), and the play fails by its insincerity. The work has been falsified to please the public—and in the end even the public is not pleased. As it is with works of art, so it is with all work. We are coming to the end of an era of civilization which began by pandering to public demand, and ended by frantically trying to create public demand for an output so false and meaningless that even a doped public revolted from the trash offered to it and plunged into war rather than swallow any more of it. The danger of "serving the community" is that one is part of the community, and that in serving it one may only be serving a kind of communal egotism. The only true way of serving the community is to be truly in sympathy with the community—to be one's self part of the community—and then to serve the work, without giving the community another thought. Then the work will endure, because it will be true to itself. It is the work that serves the community; the business of the worker is to serve the work.

Where we have become confused is in mixing up the *ends* to which our work is put with the *way* in which the work is done. The end of the work will be decided by our religious outlook: as we *are* so we *make*. It is the business of religion to make us Christian people, and then our work will naturally be turned to Christian ends, because our work is the expression of ourselves. But the *way* in which the work is done is governed by no sanction except the good of the work itself; and religion has no direct connexion with that, except to insist that the workman should be free to do his work well according to its own integrity. Jacques Maritain—one of the very few religious writers of our time who really understand the nature of creative work—has summed the matter up in a sentence:

"What is required is the perfect practical discrimination between the end pursued by the workman (*finis operantis*) and the end to be served by the work (*finis operis*), so that the workman may work for his wages but the work be controlled and set in being only in relation to its proper good and nowise in relation to the wages earned; so that the artist may work for any and every human intention he likes, but the work taken by itself be performed and constructed for its proper beauty alone."

Or perhaps we may put it more shortly still: If work is to find its right place in the world, it is the duty of the Church to see to it that the work serves God, and that the worker serves the work.

VII. The Other Six Deadly Sins *

PERHAPS the bitterest commentary on the way in which Christian doctrine has been taught in the last few centuries is the fact that to the majority of people the word "immorality" has come to mean one thing and one thing only. The name of an association like yours is generally held to imply that you are concerned to correct only one sin out of those seven which the Church recognizes as capital. By a hideous irony, our shrinking reprobation of that sin has made us too delicate so much as to name it, so that we have come to use for it the words which were made to cover the whole range of human corruption. A man may be greedy and selfish; spiteful, cruel, jealous, and unjust; violent and brutal; grasping, unscrupulous, and a liar; stubborn and arrogant; stupid, morose, and dead to every noble instinct—and still we are ready to say of him that he is not an immoral man. I am reminded of a young man who once said to me with perfect simplicity: "I did not know there were seven deadly sins: please tell me the names of the other six."

About the sin called *Luxuria* or *Lust,* I shall therefore say only three things. First, that it is a sin, and that it ought to be called plainly by its own name, and neither huddled away under a generic term like immorality, nor confused with love.

Secondly, that up till now the Church, in hunting down this sin, has had the active alliance of Caesar, who has been concerned to maintain family solidarity and the orderly devolution of property in the interests of the State. But now that contract and not status is held to be the basis of society, Caesar need no longer rely on the family to maintain social solidarity; and now that so much property is held anonymously by trusts and joint-stock companies, the

* An address delivered at Westminster, England, October 23, 1941.

63

laws of inheritance lose a great deal of their importance. Consequently, Caesar is now much less interested than he was in the sleeping arrangements of his citizens, and has in this matter cynically denounced his alliance with the Church. This is a warning against putting one's trust in any child of man—particularly in Caesar. If the Church is to continue her campaign against Lust, she must do so on her own—that is, on sacramental—grounds; and she will have to do it, if not in defiance of Caesar, at least without his assistance.

Thirdly, there are two main reasons for which people fall into the sin of Luxuria. It may be through sheer exuberance of animal spirits: in which case a sharp application of the curb may be all that is needed to bring the body into subjection and remind it of its proper place in the scheme of man's twofold nature. Or—and this commonly happens in periods of disillusionment like our own, when philosophies are bankrupt and life appears without hope—men and women may turn to lust in sheer boredom and discontent, trying to find in it some stimulus which is not provided by the drab discomfort of their mental and physical surroundings. When *that* is the case, stern rebukes and restrictions are worse than useless. It is as though one were to endeavour to cure anaemia by bleeding; it only reduces further an already impoverished vitality. The mournful and medical aspect of twentieth-century pornography and promiscuity strongly suggests that we have reached one of these periods of spiritual depression, where people go to bed because they have nothing better to do. In other words, the "regrettable moral laxity" of which respectable people complain may have its root cause not in Luxuria at all, but in some other of the sins of society, and may automatically begin to cure itself when that root cause is removed.

The Church, then, officially recognizes six other capital or basic sins—seven altogether. Of these, three may be roughly called the warm-hearted or disreputable sins, and the remaining four the cold-hearted or respectable sins. It is interesting to notice that Christ rebuked the three disreputable sins only in mild or general terms, but uttered the most violent vituperations against the respectable ones. Caesar and the Pharisees, on the other hand, strongly dislike anything warm-hearted or disreputable, and set great store by the cold-hearted and respectable sins, which they are in a conspiracy to call virtues. And we may note that, as a result of this unholy alliance between worldly interest and religious opinion, the common man is rather inclined to canonize the warm-hearted sins for himself, and to thank God openly that he is broad-minded, given to a high standard of living, and instinct with righteous indignation—not prurient, strait-laced or namby-pamby, or even as this Pharisee. It is difficult to blame the common man very much for this natural reaction against the insistent identification of Christian morality with everything that Christ most fervently abhorred.

The sin of *Ira* or *Wrath* is one, perhaps, to which the English as a nation are not greatly addicted, except in a rather specialized form. On the whole we are slow to anger, and dislike violence. We can be brutal and destructive—usually, however, only under provocation; and much of our apparent brutality is due much less to violence of temper than to sheer unimaginative stupidity (a detestable sin in itself, but quite different in nature and origin). On the whole, we are an easy-going, good-humoured people, who hate with difficulty and find it almost impossible to cherish rancour or revenge.

This is true, I think, of the English. It is perhaps not quite true of those who profess and call themselves British. The Celt is quarrelsome; he prides himself that with him it is a word and a blow. He broods upon the memory of ancient wrongs in a way that to the Englishman is incomprehensible; if the English were Irish by temperament they would still be roused to fury by the name of the Battle of Hastings, instead of summing it up philosophically as "1066 and All That." The Celt clings fiercely to his ancient tribal savageries, and his religious habits are disputatious, polemical, and (in extreme instances, as on the Irish border) disgraced by blood-thirst and a persecuting frenzy. But let the Englishman not be in too great a hurry to congratulate himself. He has one besetting weakness, by means of which he may very readily be led or lashed into the sin of Wrath: he is peculiarly liable to attacks of righteous indignation. While he is in one of these fits he will fling himself into a debauch of fury and commit extravagances which are not only evil but ridiculous.

We all know pretty well the man—or perhaps still more frequently the woman—who says that anybody who tortures a helpless animal should be flogged till he shrieks for mercy. The harsh, grating tone and the squinting, vicious countenance accompanying the declaration are enough to warn us that this righteous anger is devil-born, and trembling on the verge of mania. But we do not always recognize this ugly form of possession when it cloaks itself under a zeal for efficiency or a lofty resolution to expose scandals—particularly if it expresses itself only in print or in platform verbiage. It is very well known to the more unscrupulous part of the Press that nothing pays so well in the newspaper world as the manufacture of schism and the exploitation of wrath. Turn over the pages of the more popular papers if you want to see how avarice thrives on hatred and the passion of violence. To foment grievance and to set men at variance is the trade by which agitators thrive and journalists make money. A dog-fight, a brawl, or a war is always news; if news of that kind is lacking, it pays well to contrive it. The average English mind is a fertile field in which to sow the dragon's teeth of moral indignation; and the fight that follows will be blind, brutal, and merciless.

That is not to say that scandals should not be exposed, or that no anger is justified. But you may know the mischief-maker by the warped malignancy of his language as easily as by the warped malignancy of his face and voice. His fury is without restraint and without magnanimity—and it is aimed, not at checking the offence, but at starting a pogrom against the offender. He would rather the evil were not

cured at all than that it were cured quietly and without
violence. His evil lust of wrath cannot be sated unless somebody is hounded down, beaten, and trampled on, and a
savage war-dance executed upon the body.

I have said that the English are readily tempted into this
kind of debauch. I will add that it *is* a debauch, and, like
other debauches, leaves him with a splitting head, a bad
hang-over, and a crushing sense of shame. When he does
give way to wrath, he makes a very degrading exhibition of
himself, because wrath is a thing unnatural to him; it af-
fects him like drink or drugs. In the shame-faced mood that
follows, he becomes spiritless, sick at heart, and enfeebled
in judgment. I am therefore the more concerned about a
highly unpleasant spirit of vindictiveness that is being com-
mended to us at this moment, camouflaged as righteous
wrath and a warlike spirit. It is not a warlike spirit at
all—at any rate, it is very unlike the spirit in which soldiers
make war. The good soldier is on the whole remarkable
both for severity in his measures, and for measure in his
severity. He is as bloodthirsty as his duty requires him to
be, and, as a rule, not more. Even in Germany, the difference between the professional and the political fighter is
said to be very marked in this respect. There are, however,
certain people here whose martial howls do not suggest the
battle-cry even of a savage warrior so much as Miss Henri-
etta Petowker reciting *The Blood-Drinker's Burial* in Mrs.
Kenwigs's front parlour. If I say: "Do not listen to them,"
it is not because there is no room for indignation, but because there is a point at which righteous indignation passes
over into the deadly sin of Wrath; and once it has passed
that point, it is liable, like all other passions, to stagger
over into its own opposite, the equally fatal sin of Sloth
or Accidie, of which we shall have something to say pres-
ently. Ungovernable rage is the sin of the warm heart and
the quick spirit; in such men it is usually very quickly re-
pented of—though before that happens it may have wrought
irreparable destruction. We shall have to see to it that the
habit of wrath and destruction which war fastens upon us

is not carried over into the peace. And above all we must see to it *now* that our blind rages are not harnessed and driven by those men of the cold head and the cold heart—the Envious, the Avaricious, and the Proud.

The third warm-hearted sin is named *Gula* in Latin and in English, *Gluttony*. In its vulgarest and most obvious form we may feel that we are not much tempted to it. Certain other classes of people—not ourselves—do, of course, indulge in this disreputable kind of wallowing. Poor people of coarse and unrefined habits drink too much beer. Rich people, particularly in America and in those luxury hotels which we cannot afford, stuff themselves with food. Young people—especially girls younger than ourselves—drink far too many cocktails and smoke like chimneys. And some very reprehensible people contrive, even in war-time, to make pigs of themselves in defiance of the rationing order—like the young woman who (according to a recent gossip column) contrived to eat five separate lunches in five separate restaurants in the course of a single morning. But on the whole, England in war-time is not a place where the majority of us can very easily destroy our souls with Gluttony. We may congratulate ourselves that, if we have not exactly renounced our sins, this particular sin at any rate has renounced us.

Let us seize this breathing-space, while we are out of reach of temptation, to look at one very remarkable aspect of the sin of Gula. We have all become aware lately of something very disquieting about what we call our economic system. An odd change has come over us since the arrival of the machine age. Whereas formerly it was considered a virtue to be thrifty and content with one's lot, it is now considered to be the mark of a progressive nation that it is filled with hustling, go-getting citizens, intent on raising their standard of living. And this is not interpreted to mean merely that a decent sufficiency of food, clothes, and shelter is attainable by all citizens. It means much more and much less than this. It means that every citizen is encouraged to consider more, and more complicated, luxuries necessary to his well-being. The gluttonous consumption of manufactured goods had become, before the war, the prime civic virtue. And why? Because the machines can produce cheaply only if they produce in vast quantities; because unless the machines can produce cheaply nobody can afford to keep them running; and because, unless they are kept running, millions of citizens will be thrown out of employment, and the community will starve.   •

We need not stop now to go round and round the vicious circle of production and consumption. We need not remind ourselves of the furious barrage of advertisement by which people are flattered and frightened out of a reasonable contentment into a greedy hankering after goods which they do not really need; nor point out for the thousandth time how every evil passion—snobbery, laziness, vanity, concupiscence, ignorance, greed—is appealed to in these campaigns. Nor how unassuming communities (described as "backward countries") have these desires ruthlessly forced upon them by their neighbours in the effort to find an outlet for goods whose market is saturated. And we must not take up too much time in pointing out how, as the necessity to sell goods in quantity becomes more desperate the people's appreciation of quality is violently discouraged and suppressed. You must not buy goods that last too long, for production cannot be kept going unless the goods wear out, or fall out of fashion, and so can be thrown away and replaced with others. If a man invents anything that would give lasting satisfaction, his invention must be bought up by the manufacturer so that it may never see the light of day. Nor must the worker be encouraged to take too much interest in the thing he makes; if he did, he might desire to make it as well as it can be made, and that would not pay. It is better that he should work in a soulless indifference, even though such treatment should break his spirit, and cause him to hate his work. The difference between the factory hand and the craftsman is that the craftsman lives to do the work he loves; but the factory hand lives by doing the work he despises. The service of the machine will not have it otherwise. We know about all this, and must not discuss it now—but I will ask you to remember it.

The point I want to make *now* is this: that whether or not it is desirable to keep up this fearful whirligig of industrial finance based on gluttonous consumption, it could not be kept up for a single moment without the co-operative gluttony of the consumer. Legislation, the control of wages and profits, the balancing of exports and imports, elaborate schemes for the distribution of surplus commodities, the State ownership of enterprise, complicated systems of social credit, and finally wars and revolutions are all invoked in the hope of breaking down the thing known as the present Economic System. Now it may well be that its breakdown would be a terrific disaster and produce a worse chaos than that which went before—we need not argue about it. The point is that, without any legislation whatever, the whole system would come crashing down in a day if every consumer were voluntarily to restrict his purchases to the things he really needed. "The fact is," said a working man the other day at a meeting, "that when we fall for these advertisements we're being had for mugs." So we are. The sin of Gluttony, of Greed, of overmuch stuffing of ourselves, is the sin that has delivered us over into the power of the machine.

In evil days between the wars we were confronted with some ugly contrasts between plenty and poverty. Those contrasts should be, and must be, reduced. But let us say frankly that they are not likely to be reduced, so long as the poor admire the rich for the indulgence in precisely that gluttonous way of living which rivets on the world the chain of the present economic system, and do their best to imitate rich men's worst vices. To do that is to play into the hands of those whose interest it is to keep the system going. You will notice that, under a war economy, the contrast is being flattened out; we are being forced to reduce and regulate our personal consumption of commodities, and to revise our whole notion of what constitutes good citizenship in the financial sense. This is the judgment of this world:

when we will not amend ourselves by Grace, we are compelled under the yoke of Law. You will notice also that
we are learning certain things. There seems, for example, to
be no noticeable diminution in our health and spirits due
to the fact that we have only the choice of, say, half a dozen
dishes in a restaurant instead of forty. In the matter of
clothing, we are beginning to regain our respect for stuffs
that will wear well; we can no longer be led away by the
specious argument that it is smarter and more hygienic to
wear underlinen and stockings once and then throw them
away than to buy things that will serve us for years. We
are having to learn, painfully, to save food and material and
to salvage waste products; and in learning to do these things
we have found a curious and stimulating sense of adventure.
For it is the great curse of Gluttony that it ends by destroying all sense of the precious, the unique, the irreplaceable.
But what will happen to us when the war-machine ceases to
consume our surplus products for us? Shall we hold fast
to our rediscovered sense of real values and our adventurous
attitude of life? If so, we shall revolutionize world economy
without any political revolution. Or shall we again allow
our Gluttony to become the instrument of an economic
system that is satisfactory to nobody? That system as we
know it thrives upon waste and rubbish-heaps. At present
the waste (that is, sheer gluttonous consumption) is being
done for us in the field of war. In peace, if we do not revise our ideas, we shall ourselves become its instruments.
The rubbish-heap will again be piled on our own doorsteps,
on our own backs, in our own bellies. Instead of the wasteful consumption of trucks and tanks, metal and explosives,
we shall have back the wasteful consumption of wireless sets
and silk stockings, drugs and paper, cheap pottery and
cosmetics—all the slop and swill that pour down the sewers
over which the palace of Gluttony is built.

Gluttony is warm-hearted. It is the excess and perversion
of that free, careless, and generous mood which desires to
enjoy life and to see others enjoy it. But, like Lust and
Wrath, it is a headless, heedless sin, that puts the good-

natured person at the mercy of the cold head and the cold heart; and these exploit it and bring it to judgment, so that at length it issues in its own opposite—in that very "dearth in the midst of plenty" at which we stand horrified today.

In especial, it is at the mercy of the sin called *Avaritia* or *Covetousness*. At one time this sin was content to call itself "Honest Thrift," and under that name was, as they might say in Aberdeen, "varra weel respectit." The cold-hearted sins recommend themselves to Church and State by the restraints they lay upon the vulgar and disreputable warm-hearted sins. The thrifty poor do not swill beer in pubs, or indulge in noisy quarrels in the streets to the annoyance of decent people—moreover, they are less likely to become a burden on the rates. The thrifty well-to-do do not abash their pious neighbours by lavish indulgence in Gula or Luxuria—which are both very expensive sins. Nevertheless, there used always to be certain reservations about the respect accorded to Covetousness. It was an unromantic, unspectacular sin. Unkind people sometimes called it by rude names, such as Parsimony and Niggardliness. It was a narrow, creeping, pinched kind of sin; and it was not a good mixer. It was more popular with Caesar than with Caesar's subjects; it had no glamour about it.

It was left for the present age to endow Covetousness with glamour on a big scale, and to give it a title which it could carry like a flag. It occurred to somebody to call it Enterprise. From the moment of that happy inspiration, Covetousness has gone forward and never looked back. It has become a swaggering, swashbuckling, piratical sin, going about with its hat cocked over its eye, and with pistols tucked into the tops of its jack-boots. Its war-cries are "Business Efficiency!" "Free Competition!" "Get Out or Get Under!" and "There's Always Room at the Top!" It no longer screws and saves—it launches out into new enterprises; it gambles and speculates; it thinks in a big way; it takes risks. It can no longer be troubled to deal in real wealth, and so remain attached to Work and the Soil. It has set money free from all such hampering ties; it has interests in every